Preparation
for the
Final Crisis

Preparation
for the
Final Crisis

A compilation of passages from the Bible and the
spirit of prophecy, with comments by

Fernando Chaij

Former Book Editor of Inter-American Publications,
Spanish Division of the Pacific Press
Publishing Association

With an appendix by
M. E. LOEWEN
Former Religious Liberty Secretary of the
General Conference

Pacific Press Publishing Association
Boise, Idaho
Oshawa, Ontario, Canada

Library of Congress Catalog Card No. 66-29118
ISBN 0-8163-0137-9

In most cases the italics appearing in the quoted
matter are supplied by the author.

91 92 93 94 95 • 25 24 23 22 21

CONTENTS

KEY TO ABBREVIATIONS OF
ELLEN G. WHITE BOOK TITLES

AA   *The Acts of the Apostles* (1911)

1BC   *The Seventh-day Adventist Bible Commentary*, Vol. 1

CH   *Counsels on Health* (Compiled 1923)*

ChS   *Christian Service* (Compiled 1925)

COL   *Christ's Object Lessons* (1900)

DA   *The Desire of Ages* (1898)

Ed   *Education* (1903)

Ev   *Evangelism* (Compiled 1946)

EW   *Early Writings* (1851, 1854, 1858)

GC   *The Great Controversy* (1888, 1911)

GW   *Gospel Workers* (1915)

LS   *Life Sketches of Ellen G. White* (1915)

MYP   *Messages to Young People*

PK   *Prophets and Kings* (1917)

PP   *Patriarchs and Prophets* (1890)

RH   *Review and Herald*

SC   *Steps to Christ* (1892)

SpT   *Special Testimonies*

1SM   *Selected Messages*, Book 1 (Compiled 1958)

1T   *Testimonies*, Vol. 1 (Vols. 1-9: 1855-1909)

TM   *Testimonies to Ministers and Gospel Workers*
       (Compiled 1923)

1TT   *Testimony Treasures*, Vol. 1 (Vols. 1-3: 1855-1915)

*E. G. White books published subsequent to Mrs. White's death in 1915 are compilations from her various writings. They are released by the trustees of the White Estate in harmony with her instruction to the board of trustees, to whom she entrusted the manuscripts.

6

PREFACE

This book is dedicated to the Seventh-day Adventist Church. Its purpose is to correlate in concise, chronological form the tremendous events predicted to take place in the world and in the church just before the second coming of Christ.

The work contains many passages of Scripture and quotations from the writings of Ellen G. White, interwoven with explanations and comments to aid in understanding their relationship. Thus, directly inspired messages from God form the foundation of all that is here presented. Comments which have been added for clarification are printed in black, while the quotations from the writings of Ellen G. White are in color. An appendix especially prepared by M. E. Loewen, Public Affairs and Religious Liberty Secretary of the General Conference, has been added.

On traveling to various parts of the field, visiting churches, the compiler and author has been convinced of the immense benefit that the brethren can receive by the careful study of that which God has had written for us in this dramatic hour of history. As these vital themes were presented, the hearers as well as the speaker received new inspiration on reviewing the inspired messages for this time.

We have, then, a well-grounded conviction that the orderly analysis of these important subjects and the study of the divine messages will constitute a powerful stimulus for the reader to advance to a higher level of Christian experience in preparation for the great crisis which we expect.

The first suggestion that such a book as this should be published came from Dr. David A. DeLima, an active self-supporting missionary in the Republic of Mexico. He sent us a manuscript with a partial compilation of references from the spirit of prophecy, which we examined with interest. This prompted the Book Publishing Committee of the Pacific Press to study the idea and approve it in principle. The committee then assigned the author the task of assembling the material in documented form as we herewith present it.

In working on the project, we have consulted the pamphlet by Raymond F. Cottrell entitled *Crisis and Victory,* and the small, carefully compiled work of Robert L. Odom, *The Final Crisis and Delivery*. Other publications, including the well-documented two-volume set *Our Firm Foundation,* in which are assembled the presentations made by a number of Seventh-day Adventist scholars at the 1952 Seventh-day Adventist Bible Conference, provided helpful reference material. Our fundamental sources, however, have been the Bible and the writings of Ellen G. White.

The first chapter presents a brief survey. Here are described, as in panoramic view, the great events of the immediate future. The various incidents are then studied separately in the following chapters with ample documentation from Bible texts and Ellen G. White quotations. The latter are drawn from both her early descriptions and her later fuller presentations. See the statement "The Chronology of the Spirit of Prophecy Sources."

We are particularly grateful to a number of experienced ministers and administrators who have read the manuscript and encouraged its publication. We also acknowledge their helpful suggestions.

The Pacific Press publishes the book as a contribution to the task of guiding the advent people in their preparation to meet the Lord when He comes the second time.

FERNANDO CHAIJ.

CHRONOLOGY OF THE
SPIRIT OF PROPHECY SOURCES

Statement prepared by Arthur L. White,
Secretary to the Ellen G. White Estate

THE READER of this volume will do well to keep in mind that the scenes climaxing earth's history and presenting the experience of the faithful were portrayed repeatedly in vision to Ellen G. White over a period of many years. The initial revelations given early in her experience when the church was yet young were at times broad in scope but lacked much of the detail of later views. The Lord led His people into an understanding of the events awaiting the church only as fast as they could grasp and understand them. But in each successive vision specific areas were delineated with significant emphasis, and at times some phases were presented in very minute detail. In assembling the several accounts penned over a span of more than fifty years to form a composite picture, there emerges illuminating portrayal, but with some inevitable repetition of major points.

The first vision given to Mrs. White in December, 1844, pictured the journey of the advent people to the city of God, climaxed by their receiving the eternal reward. See *Early Writings,* pages 14-16. This gave them assurance that God was leading them. No reference was made to the crisis before them. Ten months later, in the fall of 1845, she was shown that before Christ would come again, the saints must pass through "the time of Jacob's trouble." This was a new concept and led the pioneers to study the Scriptures to find references in which the prophets of old portrayed this event which was yet future. See James White, *A Word to the Little Flock,* page 22.

Then in April, 1847, in connection with the vision which confirmed the Sabbath truth, Ellen White was shown the attempted change of the Sabbath by the papacy and the significance of the Sabbath in earth's last conflict. This aided the advent believers to see the Sabbath in the third angel's message.

See *Early Writings,* pages 32-35, "Subsequent Visions." In this presentation of less than two pages is delineated with some detail the events of the period with which this book is concerned—the events before the church in the last crisis—from the commencement of the early time of trouble to the second advent of our Lord.

Then in 1848, and again in 1858, there was depicted before Ellen White in vision, the full sweep of the events of the age-long conflict between the powers of righteousness and the powers of evil—the controversy between Christ and Satan—from the inception of sin down through time to the present and on into the future, to the new earth. This she presented to the believers in the summer of 1858 in the 219-page *Spiritual Gifts,* Volume One, bearing the title *The Great Controversy Between Christ and His Angels and Satan and His Angels.* The emphasis is on last-day events, giving a great deal of advance information which up to that time the church did not possess. This precious early volume now constitutes the last half of *Early Writings* (pages 133-295), with the last thirty pages devoted to events presented in less than two pages in the view given in 1846. See *Early Writings,* pages 34, 35.

But the church was destined to grow and with this growth was able to grasp and utilize fuller, more detailed information concerning coming events. In many visions there was opened up to Ellen White in still greater detail the entire great controversy story and especially the last crucial events of the crisis. In due time these fuller presentations were imparted to the church and the world in the 400-page *Great Controversy* in 1884, followed by an amplified, enlarged version of 700 pages in 1888. This she reissued in 1911, giving us the book we have today. In this volume the depiction of the coming crisis and final deliverance fills 100 pages. See *The Great Controversy,* pages 551-652.

Also during the years, in several chapters in the *Testimonies for the Church* and in the *Review and Herald* and other journals of the church, Ellen White made reference to the crises before us, particularly in connection with Sunday-law issues which loomed large for a decade beginning with the mid-1880's. The references are quite numerous, but the reader is directed especially to:

5T   449-554 "The Coming Crisis" (1885)
5T   711-718 "The Impending Conflict" (1889)
2SM 367-375 "Preparing for the Final Crisis" (Address
      before the General Conference Session of 1891)

One is impressed with the unity of presentation over a period of half a century, one statement complementing another. It is from these combined spirit of prophecy sources portraying coming events, some in statements of broad sweep and others in minute detail, that the quotations for this compilation have been drawn. In an endeavor to give the inspired comments in their fullness and yet to assemble them so as to outline a general picture of coming events and their approximate sequence, the compiler has condoned considerable overlapping and a repetition of main points. The reader will understand that the quotations appear in this manner to give the full picture, and he is asked to overlook the lack of smoothness in reading.

While in general the date of writing is not particularly significant, yet as a reminder that the materials have been drawn from sources penned over a period of more than half a century, the date of publication accompanies the listing of each E. G. White volume in the "Key to Abbreviations" on page 6. Volumes issued subsequent to 1915 are compilations of E. G. White materials assembled by the White Estate Trustees in harmony with Mrs. White's instructions. In a few instances where the date of writing was thought to be particularly significant, it is given in connection with the individual reference. All quotations credited to the *S.D.A. Bible Commentary* are spirit of prophecy materials drawn from the E. G. White supplements appearing at the close of each volume.

It is the settled conviction of careful students of the E. G. White writings that it is not possible from these writings to fix with precision the exact chronological position of each detail of coming events. There may be some overlapping of events in different parts of the world; there may also be some variation in sequence. Nonetheless it is important that we review these events as set before us in the Bible and the spirit of prophecy.

We believe the following point needs ever to be kept in mind by the reader: Denominational policy calls for the compiler of a collection of E. G. White statements to submit the manuscript to the E. G. White Estate before taking steps to publish the compilation. This the present compiler has done. However, it does not therefore follow that the publication of this book indicates that the White Estate sponsors or endorses this book. The Estate never assumes sponsorship of this type of publication. At most the White Estate declares that it offers no objection to the publication of the passages from the E. G. White writings in the order given. Responsibility for this book or any similar book, rightfully rests with the compiler and the publishers.

How fortunate Seventh-day Adventists are to have provided for them, in the spirit of prophecy, windows through which we may gain clear views of what awaits the church and the world. These scenes of the climax of the great controversy, along with views given in the Word of God, offer a rewarding field for study.

INTRODUCTION

A Panoramic View of the Final Events

THE WORLD today finds itself near the end of its long and eventful history. God has favored His people with wonderful prophetic revelations of the hour in which we live, showing the development of divine plans and pointing out great events of the future. Some of these messages He gave through the inspired pen of Ellen G. White. They amplify the prophecies of the Bible, open before us a vast panorama of coming events, and urge us to obtain the preparation we need for the great approaching crisis.

"KNOWING THE TIME"

Paul rightly says: "That, knowing the time, that now it is high time to awake out of sleep: for now is our salvation nearer than when we believed." Romans 13:11. These words apply with peculiar force to the advent people.

While the world shakes with fear for the uncertainty of tomorrow, we may know the times.

Any international traveler carries an itinerary and a map. He knows which parts of the trip he has already covered and which stops remain to be made. He knows ahead of time the day and hour of his arrival at each of the airports. By his careful attention to detail, the whole itinerary works out with precision.

The children of God on their marvelous trip toward the final goal, also have a map, an excellent one—the Bible—and a precise itinerary—the inspired prophecies.

STAGES ALREADY COMPLETED

Looking backward, the faithful gain confidence when they observe how predictions made thousands of years ago have been fulfilled exactly.

The four ancient world empires arose and disappeared as foretold in the prophecies of Daniel 2 and 7. The iron Roman Empire was split up into the nations of modern Europe, which today remain divided despite all attempts to reunite them—just as symbolized by the clay and the iron in the feet and toes of the image.

The 1260 years of papal supremacy, now history, stand as another testimony of the surety of the everlasting prophetic gift.

One of the heads of the first beast of Revelation 13 received a mortal wound, but it was also healed—all according to divine prophecy. Today we witness the fulfilling of the last part of that prophecy as we see the whole world beginning to wonder after the beast.

The happenings predicted by the longest and most striking time prophecy of the Bible, the 2300 days of Daniel 8:14, with its seventy weeks included in Daniel 9, have come true with astonishing accuracy. The return of the Jews from Persia to Jerusalem, the rebuilding of the city and the wall, the baptism of Jesus, and the death of the Saviour on Calvary, occurred with mathematical precision as the inspired oracle foretold.

And when the close of this period arrived, one of the greatest events of religious history took place. In fulfillment of the prophecies of Daniel 8 and 9 and Revelation 14, the advent movement arose, exactly on time, to preach the message of judgment and the everlasting gospel in its modern form, "the present truth."

Signs in the heavens predicted by the Lord Jesus in His prophetic sermon two thousand years ago—the darkening of the sun and moon and the falling of the stars—came to pass more than a century ago. Conditions today in the social, political, and religious world are fulfilling Bible prophecy with dramatic accuracy. The increase in immorality and delinquency, fear that is drying human hearts, wars and rumors of wars, increasing frequency of earthquakes, false prophets and spurious religious movements, signs and wonders accomplished by the power of the enemy—all eloquently proclaim that we are living in the last hour, when the world and the church will witness the greatest events in history.

Prodigious growth in scientific knowledge, so rapid that the most extraordinary inventions or discoveries surprise no one anymore, tell the same story. Constantly accelerating speeds of travel, accentuated by modern man's conquest of space, are fulfilling the prediction of the prophet Daniel that knowledge would be increased and men would run to and fro. See Daniel 12:4.

A look backward, in other words, convinces us that Bible prophecy has been fulfilled with amazing precision, that its longest prophetic time period ended in 1844, and that now only the events of the last days climaxed by the glorious return of Jesus in the clouds of heaven await us.

But before God's redeemed arrive at their desired goal, the Word of God and the testimonies of Ellen G. White point out that a combination of events of great magnitude will soon come to pass in rapid succession—events which will catapult the church into the midst of a great crisis. For this each individual believer needs special preparation.

The past confirms our confidence in the future. The exactitude with which each one of the events in the prophecies has been fulfilled to our day, assures us that events still future will come to pass.

The wonderful way in which God has guided and protected His people through the centuries, overruling the designs of evil powers, indicates that the church, now militant, will continue to be guided until it soon becomes the church triumphant. "We have nothing to fear for the future, except as we shall forget the way the Lord has led us, and His teaching in our past history." —LS 196.

A PANORAMA OF THE FUTURE

With this confidence, with this surety, let us now survey the immediate future, extending our gaze as far as the return of Christ. Let us, in panoramic vision, pick out the events which will confront us as a people until the day of our final liberation.

In the following chapters we will see these events in detail as described by inspired words. But first a summary—a general view of the whole. This will help us to establish the right relationship between one situation and another.

Before probation ends, while men can yet accept the provisions of the gospel, the following events will occur: the sealing, the latter rain, the loud cry, the finishing of the work, the shaking time. Listing these events in this order does not imply they

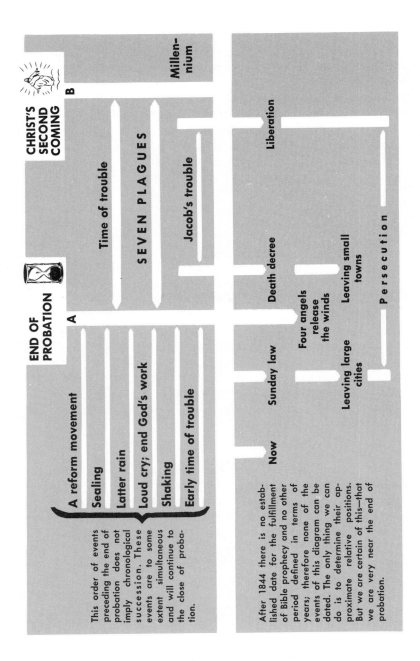

END OF PROBATION

CHRIST'S SECOND COMING

A reform movement
Sealing
Latter rain
Loud cry; end God's work
Shaking
Early time of trouble

Time of trouble

SEVEN PLAGUES

A

B

Millennium

This order of events preceding the end of probation does not imply chronological succession. These events are to some extent simultaneous and will continue to the close of probation.

Now

Sunday law

Death decree

Jacob's trouble

Liberation

Leaving large cities

Four angels release the winds

Leaving small towns

Persecution

After 1844 there is no established date for the fulfillment of Bible prophecy and no other period defined in terms of years; therefore none of the events of this diagram can be dated. The only thing we can do is to determine their approximate relative positions. But we are certain of this—that we are very near the end of probation.

will occur in this chronological sequence. Some or all of them may be simultaneous. We know that when the decree of Revelation 22:11 is pronounced, and probation closes, these events will also have ended. Thus the way will have been cleared for the beginning of the great time of trouble.

But accompanying these events and in a sense preparing the way for them, there will occur within the church of God a true movement of reform. To a great extent it will come about as a result of the message of the True Witness to Laodicea and of the church's understanding and reception of the great subject of righteousness by faith. This will cause a spiritual awakening and renewal of life. It will hasten the falling of the latter rain and the proclamation of the message to prepare a people for the time of trouble and the majestic appearance of Christ.

The sealing. In order to prepare His children for the time of trouble, God desires to stamp upon them the seal of His law, of His character, and of His perfection. The process, which is taking place now, will soon be over. Actually, the sealing concerns individuals and can be described as a process which starts at conversion and ends with the close of probation, whether at the death of the believer or at the end of the investigative judgment. Only those who are prepared can be sealed, and only those who are sealed can pass successfully through the time of trouble and enter into the presence of the Lord at His second coming. The preparation consists of cleansing from sin, and victory over every weakness and defect.

The latter rain, the loud cry, and the finishing of the work. To hasten the completion of the gospel commission, God desires to pour out on His people the latter rain of the Holy Spirit. Thus as the early rain prepared the apostolic church to proclaim the good news of salvation with success and efficiency in all parts of their world, so this outpouring of divine power will enable the people of God today to complete the unfinished work and to reach every nation, tribe, tongue, and people with the last evangelic message. The promise of the latter rain is for today, not for some future time. But an indispensable prerequisite for its fulfillment is that the great majority of church members consecrate themselves completely to God, denying self, repudiating sin in all its forms, and seeking the Lord with humility.

Shortly the loud cry of the message must be given. Accompanied by a manifestation of divine power, the earth will be lighted with the glory of the Lord, and the work will be finished according to the plan and promise of God. See Revelation 18:1-4.

A special process of reform and sanctification will be needed among the ranks of the church—which will affect the great majority of the members—in preparation for the latter rain, the loud cry, and the finishing of the gospel task.

The shaking. The shaking is another of the great events which will affect the church during the time of grace (probation). This term suggests that some who are numbered among the people of God will apostatize. Many Adventists will leave the ranks because they did not accept with all their hearts the divine call to conversion and complete consecration, and because they rejected the message of Christ to the church of Laodicea—a message of repentance and reform of life—maintaining only a formal and superficial experience.

When the great hour of crisis for the church arrives and persecution begins with the enforcement of a general Sunday law, many will desert, and some will become our worst enemies. Only a complete surrender of life to God and a constant experience of growing in grace will safeguard us from this great danger and will maintain us united with the host of consecrated men and women who will gloriously triumph when Jesus appears.

The early time of trouble. The last hours of probationary time will be tempestuous and difficult for the world in general, and also for the children of God. In the world, even while the four angels are holding the winds, war, confusion, political problems, economic and social distress, disintegration of the family, fear, and worry will increase.

Governments, although they may try very hard, will not be able to cope with the complex problems confronting them. This early time of trouble, to which Jesus referred in Luke 21:25, comes before the great time of trouble which will begin as soon as probation closes.

For God's people the early time of trouble will be made more serious by persecution, to which they will be subjected by apostate powers. Nevertheless, God will be with them to fortify them and help them to live triumphantly and suffer gladly for His sake. "Because thou hast kept the word of My patience," promises the Lord to the persecuted, "I also will keep thee from the hour of temptation, which shall come upon all the world, to try them that dwell upon the earth. Behold, I come quickly: hold that fast which thou hast, that no man take thy crown." Revelation 3:10, 11.

The persecution. In Revelation 13:11-17 is given a prophetic description of persecution, which the spirit of prophecy has amplified. This persecution will begin before the close of probation and will become more intense afterward, particularly during the time of Jacob's trouble. But the hour of liberation will come.

The second beast of Revelation 13, the one with horns like a lamb, represents the United States of America, a young nation, composed of a people who love liberty—a democratic country governed by a model constitution with admirable safeguards for human rights and freedom, especially freedom of conscience.

This country has fulfilled until now—and still continues to fulfill—a truly historic mission. Having achieved the highest type of religious liberty with the First Amendment to its Constitution—which prohibits legislation by Congress on religious matters—it established a complete and respectful separation of church and state and became a bulwark of liberty of conscience. To its hospitable shores persecuted men and women from all parts of the world have come, seeking refuge under the guarantees of this wonderful political system.

In His providence God chose the United States in which to establish the center of the world work of Seventh-day Adventists. Thus, without restraint, means and missionaries have gone out through the years from this rich, progressive, and liberty-loving country to carry the threefold evangelistic message to the four corners of the earth.

Nevertheless, the prophecy affirms that this country, represented by the lamblike beast, will change its nature completely, and as a result will commit the following acts:

1. It will speak as a dragon. Verse 11. And the dragon of Revelation 12 is a persecuting power.

2. It will oblige all that dwell on the earth to worship the first beast, that is to say, Rome. Verse 12. It will oblige all humanity to render obedience to a religiopolitical power and will issue injunctions of a religious character. This cancels all religious liberty maintained up to this time and inaugurates a time of coercion and persecution.

3. It will work great wonders to deceive, even to making fire come down from heaven. Verses 13, 14. This will take place because of the extraordinary prominence spiritism has achieved and because of its union with Protestantism and Catholicism.

4. It will command all those who dwell on the earth to make an image to the first beast of Revelation 13, that is, to the Roman power. Verse 14. Since this beast persecuted the saints, the image to the beast will be another power doing the same thing. This "image to the beast," as we shall see in a later chapter, is a federation of Protestant churches that will finally apostatize and unite in demanding from the state civil power to impose religious laws.

5. It will cause all to receive "the mark of the beast," forbidding anyone to buy or sell unless he has it. Verses 16, 17. Although "not all in regard to this matter is yet understood, nor will it be understood until the unrolling of the scroll," "the mark of the beast is exactly what it has been proclaimed to be." —6T 17. "The mark of the beast is . . . the observance of the first day of the week."—8T 117.

Since the mark or seal of God is the divine law, and particularly the Sabbath, the true day of rest, the mark of the beast must be a false day of rest. We know that the observance of the Sabbath, in harmony with the fourth commandment, testifies to our loyalty to God as our Creator and Saviour and to His government. Similarly the forced observance of Sunday—which will be universally imposed by the image to the beast and other apostate powers—is to a certain extent the mark of the beast, or the sign of loyalty to a false power which is an enemy of God and truth.

Finally the focal point of the great and long controversy between truth and error, between Christ and Satan, will be the observance or the violation of the true day of rest.

Those who refuse to accept the sign or mark of the beast,

those who refuse to observe Sunday or participate in acts of worship that violate the holy Sabbath, will be persecuted. They will be denied protection by the state. Constitutional guarantees will be suspended for them, and they will be deprived of the most essential rights, even those basic to life itself such as the right to buy and sell.

Before probation ends, the United States of America will pass a national Sunday law. Thus will begin a time of great trial for the church, the greatest crisis in its history.

Today laws that legislate Sunday rest pretend to be of a social and health character and allow for exceptions. People who favor them insist that they are divested of all religious intent. Such laws exist in many states of the Union.

But soon these laws will be enforced throughout the nation by Federal legislation. The enactment will probably be religious in nature, involving in some way an act of worship that would violate the true day of rest. Its passage will be demanded by the image of the beast (confederacy of apostate Protestantism in league with the state), with the full support of Catholics and spiritualists. This will start the great persecution. The movement will soon spread to other countries of the world, where similar laws will be put into effect, thus making oppression of the Sabbath-keeping minority universal.

This will be the signal for the children of God still living in large cities to leave them, and for those in small towns to prepare to leave soon.

When the seven last plagues begin to fall, that is, after the close of probation, or during the great time of trouble, the next event in the series follows:

6. The image to the beast will try to kill all those who do not worship the beast and his image. Verse 15. A death decree will be issued against those who observe the Sabbath. They will be cited as enemies of law and order and the cause of all the calamities that are devastating the earth—the plagues.

A specific date for executing the decree will be set. When this is announced, the children of God will flee from all populated centers, including small towns, and will seek refuge in forests, deserts, and rocky places, where they will enjoy the special protection of God. Heavenly angels will provide them food. This will be a time of great trouble in which the faithful will cry to God unceasingly for deliverance.

The powers allied in the war against God, His truth, and His people will be the dragon, the beast, and the false prophet. Revelation 16:13. The *dragon* represents Satan, in this particular case working by means of spiritualism in all its forms —pagan (acting in its pagan forms of worship and superstition); Christian (amalgamating itself with Protestant and Catholic worship by means of miracles and on the basis of the commonly accepted doctrine of the immortality of the soul); et cetera. The *beast* symbolizes the papacy, or the Roman Catholic Church; and the *false prophet,* apostate Protestantism. And as such, Protestantism with the papacy will act in close accord with the state to impose laws of a religious character. And this union of church and state will spread throughout the world.

Armageddon. The next act in the drama will be Armageddon, the final conflict between good and evil as described under the sixth plague. The prophet saw coming out of the mouth of the dragon (spiritism), the beast (the papacy), and the false prophet (apostate Protestantism) three unclean spirits, which are spirits of devils, which will work great signs to deceive and will go to the kings of the earth to induce them to fight this final battle against God, His people, and His truth. Revelation 16:12-14.

While persecution lasts, the faithful will be under the special protection of the Lord and His holy angels. In their last emergency flight from the cities they will be attacked by pursuing armies, but the swords raised against them will fall powerless as straws. Angels will defend the fugitives, appearing as powerful warriors. In a miraculous way bread and water will be provided for them in the wilderness.

On the very day set for the carrying out of the death sentence, the Lord will deliver the faithful. He will paralyze the wicked with a great commotion in the heavens and the earth and with an extraordinary display of the natural elements. In the midst of the confusion and wrath, the attackers will begin to fight among themselves, destroying each other. At this time the voice of God is heard, a special resurrection takes place, and a little afterward the majestic sight of the Son of God appears in the heavens.

The time of trouble. This time is described in Daniel 12:1: "At that time shall Michael stand up, the great Prince which standeth for the children of thy people: and there shall be a time of trouble, such as never was since there was a nation even to that same time: and at that time thy people shall be delivered, everyone that shall be found written in the book."

This begins when probation closes. The shaking has terminated. The refreshing from the presence of God in the latter rain has descended. The preaching of the gospel has concluded. Then Michael, that is, Christ, the great Prince who intercedes for us in the heavenly sanctuary, will "stand up" and cease His intercessory work. He will take off His priestly vestments to put on His royal robe. The heavenly temple will fill with smoke, and no one will be able to enter it.

The four angels of Revelation 7, who were holding the winds of strife, will now release them. Unrestrained, evil men will give full sway to furious human passions. And the seven last plagues will descend upon the unrighteous.

This will be a time of terrible agony for the world. Scourges such as men have never seen will ravish the earth. But for the fact that these plagues are not universal, the entire world would be depopulated.

Although the children of God will be shielded from the plagues, yet for them also this will be a time of indescribable trouble, in two ways. First, it will be a time of material trouble because of the pitiless persecution heaped upon them. Some will lose their liberty and pass days in prison cells. A great number of them will walk as fugitives in faraway places. Although defended and helped by angels, whose presence transforms even their prisons to mansions of light, they undergo severe physical hardships.

But they will also suffer terrible mental anxiety. During this time they will have no Mediator. If they had any unconfessed sins or unpardoned faults in their lives, they would be overwhelmed. They pass through an hour of uncertainty and affliction. For a little while they seem to be unsure that all their sins have been blotted out. As Jacob in the night of trouble on the banks of Jabbok, they humble their souls before God. Although their faith is severely tried, they are fortified by this extraordinary experience. Finally their prayers are answered, and they obtain peace. They cannot remember any sins that are not confessed and repented of. Before the close of probation they obtained by divine power the victory over evil, and they have been sealed. Their salvation is assured.

Between the liberation and the second coming of Christ. At the majestic intervention of God which paralyzes the wicked in their attempts to destroy the faithful, the sun shines at midnight and a frightening display of supernatural phenomena occurs. The sea boils and swells, and a terrible earthquake sends gigantic buildings crashing to ruins.

It is then that the partial resurrection occurs: The sepulchers are opened, and many of the saints are raised to be witnesses of the coming of Christ, but especially all those who have died in the faith of the third angel's message. Daniel 12:2; Revelation 1:7. Also those who pierced the Lord Jesus come out of their tombs, as well as the strongest enemies of the truth. Revelation 1:7. While the wicked are full of fear, the saints jubilantly exclaim: "Lo, this is our God; we have waited for Him, and He will save us." Isaiah 25:9.

Upon recognizing that they have been deceived, the lost begin to accuse each other. Especially do they accuse the false pastors of the flock. And the swords that they had intended to use against the saints they now use against each other. Soon these attacks are turned against the great church, against Babylon (Revelation 17:16), which will be destroyed and cut in pieces. In connection with these events the voice of God proclaims the day and the hour of Christ's coming.

The majestic appearance of Christ. The final moment of the ages has arrived, the time so long heralded by the prophets. A small black cloud appears in the heavens, and, as it approaches the earth, it becomes lighter and more brilliant, until in time it is seen to be a radiant company of angels who escort the King of kings and Lord of lords in His triumphal procession toward the earth. Christ descends, enveloped in flames of fire. The heavens roll back as a scroll. The earth trembles. The mountains are moved.

While the great celestial procession draws ever closer, a powerful earthquake shakes the earth, and the voice of Christ wakes the sleeping saints to life immortal. The living righteous are translated. Those wicked still living are destroyed by the splendor of the divine glory.

The long time of waiting has ended. The night of affliction has turned at last to glorious day. And now all the family of God on earth, redeemed by the precious blood of the Lamb, are united with their beloved Lord and Master and their heavenly Father.

Thousands of years of hopes have been fulfilled in one eternal morning of triumphant reality. You and I must be there. Now is the day of sanctification; tomorrow will be that of glorification.

CHAPTER 1

REFORM MOVEMENT
WITHIN THE CHURCH

*Need for reform—Characteristics of the reform—The heart
of the reformation: the proclamation of the Laodicean message and justification by faith—The secret of victory—
Conclusion.*

SOME twenty-seven centuries ago, the inspired prophet Joel,
under divine inspiration, referred thus to the day of God: "Blow
ye the trumpet in Zion, and sound an alarm in My holy mountain: let all the inhabitants of the land tremble: for the day
of the Lord cometh, for it is nigh at hand; a day of darkness
and of gloominess, a day of clouds and of thick darkness, as the
morning spread upon the mountains." Joel 2:1, 2.

It is true that these words had an immediate historical application in Old Testament times, when Israel was about to be in-
vaded by an enemy people. But the words were also preserved
because they refer to the time of the end, the "day of the Lord,"
the eve of the return of Christ to earth. The message calls for
the sound of a trumpet in Zion, that is, the church. It is to
spread an alarm in the holy mountain of God, that is, among
His people.

"Therefore also now, saith the Lord," the prophet continues,
"turn ye even to Me with all your heart, and with fasting, and
with weeping, and with mourning: and rend your heart, and
not your garments, and turn unto the Lord your God. . . . Blow
the trumpet in Zion, sanctify a fast, call a solemn assembly:
gather the people, sanctify the congregation. . . . Let the priests,
the ministers of the Lord, weep between the porch and the altar,
and let them say, Spare Thy people, O Lord." Verses 12-17.

In view of the earth-shaking events that are about to occur

in "the day of the Lord," church members must be awakened by a voice of alarm; they must seek a profound and genuine conversion—one of all the heart. In other words, a spiritual reformation must be effected in the church in preparation for the great events of the time of the end.

There is no doubt that we have already arrived at the very eve of the supreme hour. Therefore this call to genuine conversion and complete reformation of the life must resound now throughout the whole circumference of Zion.

This is what the Lord's messenger wrote many years ago, as the following paragraphs show:

NEED FOR REFORM

"*A revival of true godliness among us is the greatest and most urgent of all our needs. To seek this should be our first work.* There must be earnest effort to obtain the blessing of the Lord, not because God is not willing to bestow His blessing upon us, but because we are unprepared to receive it. Our heavenly Father is more willing to give His Holy Spirit to them that ask Him, than are earthly parents to give good gifts to their children. But it is our work, by confession, humiliation, repentance, and earnest prayer, to fulfill the conditions upon which God has promised to grant us His blessing." —1SM 121.

"God's people will not endure the test unless there is *a revival and a reformation.* The Lord will not admit into the mansions He is preparing for the righteous, one soul who is self-sufficient."—7T 285.

"*A reformation is needed among the people,* but it should first begin its purifying work with the ministers."—1T 469.

"Let there be a *reformation* among the people of God."—*Messages to Young People,* page 317.

"*A revival and a reformation must take place* under the ministration of the Holy Spirit. Revival and reformation are two different things. Revival signifies a renewal of spiritual life, a quickening of the powers of mind and heart, a resurrection from the spiritual death. Reformation signifies a reorganization, a change in ideas and theories, habits and practices. Reformation will not bring forth the good fruit of righteousness unless it is connected with the revival of the Spirit. Revival and reformation are to do their appointed work, and in doing this work they must blend."—ChS 42.

"I have been deeply impressed by scenes that have recently passed before me in the night season. There seemed to be a great movement—*a work of revival*—going forward in many places. Our people were moving into line, responding to God's call. My brethren, the Lord is speaking to us. Shall we not heed His voice? Shall we not trim our lamps and act like men who look for their Lord to come? The time is one that calls for light bearing, for action."—3TT 441.

"Before the final visitation of God's judgments upon the earth *there will be among the people of the Lord such a revival of primitive godliness* as has not been witnessed since apostolic times. The Spirit and power of God will be poured out upon His children."—GC 464.

CHARACTERISTICS OF THE REFORM

But Satan has been working vigorously to counterfeit the genuine spiritual reformation which the Lord desires to effect in His church. This has been the method of the great enemy since the days of antiquity: to adulterate the truth and offer falsehood, in order to cause confusion, chaos, and ruin instead of true conversion.

Satanic counterfeits of reform

Declares the inspired pen:

"In every revival he [Satan] is ready to bring in those who are unsanctified in heart and unbalanced in mind. . . .

"In all the history of the church no reformation has been carried forward without encountering serious obstacles. Thus it was in Paul's day. Wherever the apostle raised up a church, there were some who professed to receive the faith, but who brought in heresies, that, if received, would eventually crowd out the love of the truth."—GC 396.

"The seed which Luther had sown sprang up everywhere. . . .

"He [Satan] now attempted what he has attempted in every other reformatory movement—to deceive and destroy the people by palming off upon them a counterfeit in place of the true work. As there were false christs in the first century of the Christian church, so there arose false prophets in the sixteenth century."—GC 186.

Just as he has done in times past, the father of all lies has been doing in our day. Even now he is determined to disorganize the advent movement and confuse the children of God.

This is how, during our brief history as a movement, particularly in recent years, groups have sprung up bringing in disharmony and disunion. Led by men calling themselves "reformers," they destroy instead of build. Their work has not stood the Bible test: "Ye shall know them by their fruits." Matthew 7:16.

The spirit of discord and strife

A common feature of false reform movements is the spirit of discord, strife, revolution, and destructive criticism, particularly of church leaders. The spirit of prophecy advises:

"The time has come for a thorough reformation to take place. When this reformation begins, *the spirit of prayer will actuate every believer* and *will banish from the church the spirit of discord and strife*."—8T 251, (ChS 42).

In other words, the first thing accomplished by true reformation is the elimination of discord, criticism, and strife.

In describing several false reform movements, the messenger of the Lord says this of the leader of one:

"He thought God had passed all the leading workers and given him the message." Then she declared that she "attempted to show him that he was mistaken."—2SM 64.

Of another she wrote:

"He said the leaders in the church would all fall through self-exaltation, and another class of humble men would come to the front, who would do wonderful things. . . . He claimed to believe the testimonies. He claimed them to be true, and used them . . . to give force and appearance of truth to his claims."—2SM 64, 65.

But of this man and his message she wrote:

"The word of God came from God to me, 'Believe them not, I have not sent them!' " And she told him that his "message was not of God; but was deceiving the unwary."—2SM 64.

Of still another who claimed a special message she wrote:

"The same accusing spirit was with them—that is, that the church was all wrong and God was calling out a people who would work miracles."—2SM 66.

Whenever any so-called reform movement excites a spirit of destructive criticism against the leaders of the work and against the organization of the church, spreading discord and strife, we

have a sure sign, without further analysis, that Satan heads it
and that it is a counterfeit of genuine reformation.

Such movements, in order to gain followers, at first pretend
to belong to the advent people and to manifest zeal for the work
of God. But always in the end they split off into separate groups.
But for a while, until their true nature is unmasked, they cause
endless trouble and mislead sincere persons who are insufficiently
grounded.

Satan acts with energy and deceit

"At every revival of God's work the prince of evil is aroused to
more intense activity; he is now putting forth his utmost efforts for a
final struggle against Christ and His followers."—GC 593.

"*Let the people of God* arouse out of sleep and *begin in earnest
the work of repentance and reformation;* let them search the Scriptures to learn the truth as it is in Jesus; let them make an entire
consecration to God, and *evidence will not be wanting that Satan
is still active and vigilant.* With all possible deception he will manifest his power, calling to his aid all the fallen angels of his realm."
—GC 398.

Fanaticism

Among the means the devil uses to disrupt God's plan to proclaim and produce a reformation among His people, is fanaticism. He used this in the days of the apostles and during the
Protestant Reformation—in fact, in all religious revivals.

"*Fanaticism will appear in the very midst of us.* Deceptions will
come, and of such a character that if it were possible they would
mislead the very elect."—2SM 16.

"*Luther* also suffered great perplexity and distress from the
course of *fanatical persons.* . . . And the Wesleys, and others who
blessed the world by their influence and their faith, encountered at
every step the wiles of Satan in pushing overzealous, unbalanced,
and unsanctified ones into fanaticism of every grade.

"William Miller had no sympathy with those influences that led
to fanaticism. He declared, with Luther, that every spirit should be
tested by the Word of God. . . .

"In the days of the Reformation its enemies charged all the
evils of fanaticism upon the very ones who were laboring most
earnestly against it. A similar course was pursued by the opposers
of the advent movement."—GC 396, 397.

We should be on guard, however, lest undue sensitivity to charges of fanaticism lead us to resist the true revival, the genuine reformation that contains the characteristics which will be described later.

"When the Lord works through human instrumentalities, when men are moved with power from on high, Satan leads his agents to cry, 'Fanaticism!' and to warn people not to go to extremes. Let all be careful how they raise this cry; for *though there is counterfeit coin, this does not lower the value of that which is genuine.* Because there are spurious revivals and spurious conversions, it does not follow that all revivals are to be held in suspicion. Let us not show the contempt manifested by the Pharisees when they said, 'This man receiveth sinners' (Luke 15:2)."—GW 170.

"New light"

Another way the archenemy seeks to trap incautious souls is through the proclamation of so-called "new light." This observation does not, of course, indict legitimate amplification of fundamental doctrines already firmly established or clearer understanding of unfolding prophecies. But we must keep in mind the following instruction:

"When the power of God testifies as to what is truth, that truth is to stand forever as the truth. No after suppositions contrary to the light God has given are to be entertained."—1SM 161.

Authentic new light must have the following elements of identification:

1. *It will be 100 percent in accord with the Word of God,* and it will not depend on any whimsical and unbalanced interpretation of Scripture.

"Men and women will arise professing to have some new light or some new revelation whose *tendency is to unsettle faith in the old landmarks.* Their doctrines *will not bear the test of God's Word,* yet souls will be deceived."—5T 295 (2TT 107).

2. *It will not contradict any of the basic truths already established* as immovable pillars in the doctrinal structure of the church.

"He [God] does not give one man *new light contrary to the established faith of the body.* In every reform men have arisen making this claim."—5T 291 (2TT 103).

3. *Those who proclaim the new light will not be infatuated with the idea that they are superior to their brethren, and that God has chosen them, bypassing His people.* This, in general, is the exalted view leaders of so-called "reform movements" hold of themselves.

"God has not passed His people by and *chosen one solitary man* here and another there as the *only ones worthy to be entrusted with His truth."—Ibid.*

"Let none be self-confident, as though God had given them special light above their brethren. Christ is represented as dwelling in His people."—*Ibid.*

Additional characteristics of genuine reformation:

1. A spirit of prayer.
2. A spirit of sincere conversion.
3. A widespread spirit of self-denying missionary work.
4. A spirit of praise and thanksgiving.

These points have been gleaned from the following inspired paragraph:

"In visions of the night, representations passed before me of a great reformatory movement among God's people. Many were praising God. The sick were healed, and other miracles were wrought. *A spirit of intercession was seen,* even as was manifested before the great Day of Pentecost. *Hundreds and thousands were seen visiting families and opening before them the Word of God.* Hearts were convicted by the power of the Holy Spirit, and a *spirit of genuine conversion was manifest.* On every side doors were thrown open to the proclamation of the truth. The world seemed to be lightened with the heavenly influence. Great blessings were received by the true and humble people of God. *I heard voices of thanksgiving and praise, and there seemed to be a reformation* such as we witnessed in 1844."—9T 126 (3TT 345).

THE HEART OF THE REFORMATION:
THE PROCLAMATION OF THE LAODICEAN MESSAGE
AND JUSTIFICATION BY FAITH

Reformation in the church will result from the wholehearted acceptance of the message of the Faithful Witness to the church of Laodicea. It is this message of Christ to His church which will break up the pride and deceitfulness of self-righteousness and self-sufficiency, and which will produce a spirit of sincere repentance and confession. It will lead the contrite soul to the foot of the cross for cleansing from sin and the gift of Christ's righteousness.

In the hour of crisis through which the church will pass, no one can remain neutral. Luke 11:23. Positive acceptance of this frank message of love (Revelation 3:14-22) will bring blessed results in the life: genuine conversion, separation from the world, victory over the flesh, and new life from above. This is the essence of the genuine reformation that must operate in the church—in each individual heart.

Those who reject the message and prefer to remain lukewarm, formal, and filled with self-righteousness, will be shaken out in the time of sifting and will perish. The messenger of the Lord explains:

"I asked the meaning of the shaking I had seen and was shown that it would be caused by the straight testimony called forth by the counsel of the True Witness to the Laodiceans. This will have its effects upon the heart of the receiver, and will lead him to exalt the standard and pour forth the straight truth. Some will not bear this straight testimony. They will rise up against it, and this is what will cause a shaking among God's people."—EW 270.

What vital consequences hang on how the message is received—the destiny of the church! It must cause a profound repentance. All those who receive it will be purified.

"I saw that the testimony of the True Witness has not been half heeded. The solemn testimony upon which the destiny of the church hangs has been lightly esteemed, if not entirely disregarded. This testimony must work deep repentance; all who truly receive it will obey it and be purified."—EW 270.

A frank message of love

"And unto the angel of the church of the Laodiceans write; These things saith the Amen, the faithful and true Witness, the beginning of the creation of God; I know thy works, that thou art neither cold nor hot: I would thou wert cold or hot." Revelation 3:14, 15.

"The message to the church of the Laodiceans is a startling denunciation, and is applicable to the people of God at the present time."—3T 252.

The author of the message is none other than Christ, our Saviour and best Friend. He is true and faithful. He loves us, but He does not flatter us, because He desires our salvation. He speaks to us with love and sincerity. The message is straight, but it is full of mercy.

He says to us, "I know your works." One speaks to us who knows us better than we know ourselves, because the human heart is deceitful. Jeremiah 17:9. Particularly because of self-deceit found in Laodicea, He regards this message necessary for us. Therefore, since only God knows us, our attitude in the face of this message should be that of the psalmist: "Search me, O God, and know my heart: . . . and see if there be any wicked way in me, and lead me in the way everlasting." Psalm 139: 23, 24.

This message has an individual application. The Faithful Witness speaks in the singular. And the collective result in the church will be determined by the way each member responds to it and practices it.

"Thou art lukewarm"

What is it that the One who knows our hearts says? "Thou art neither cold nor hot: I would thou wert cold or hot. So then because thou art lukewarm, . . . I will spew thee out of My mouth." Revelation 3:15, 16.

Early in the experience of the church the solemn word came to us:

"The Laodicean message applies to the people of God who profess to believe present truth. The greater part are lukewarm professors, having a name but no zeal. . . . The term 'lukewarm' is applicable to this class. They profess to love the truth, yet are deficient in Christian fervor and devotion. They dare not give up wholly and run the risk of the unbeliever, yet they are unwilling to die to self and follow out closely the principles of their faith. . . .

"They do not engage thoroughly and heartily in the work of God, identifying themselves with its interests; but they hold aloof and are ready to leave their posts when their worldly personal interests demand it. The internal work of grace is wanting in their hearts."—4T 87, 88 (1TT 476, 477).

Thank God many, because of having permitted the Spirit to do His work in their lives, do not participate in this condition of lukewarmness. But one cannot help being grieved by the realization that a large part of Laodicea is made up of luke-warm ones who only profess the truth. This establishes the necessity of a definite reformation.

There are four elements that make up this lukewarmness:

1. They *"are deficient in Christian fervor and devotion."* We must live daily a life of communion with God, a life of prayer and study of the Word. Thus we satisfy our spiritual needs through the power of God—an urgent matter.

2. *"They are unwilling to die to self and follow out closely the principles of their faith."* Halfway conversion will never save us. "Turn ye even to Me with all your heart," says the Lord. A divided heart will not give us victory. Christ requires complete possession. Self must die in order for Christ to reign on the throne of the heart.

3. *"They do not engage thoroughly and heartily in the work of God, identifying themselves with its interests."* They do not dedicate sufficient time, interest, work, and resources to the cause of God.

4. *"The internal work of grace is wanting in their hearts."* God desires to perform this miracle in every heart, and in a complete way. "He which hath begun a good work in you," says Paul, "will perform it until the day of Jesus Christ." Philippians 1:6. Thank God that He wants to do it and that He can do it! But our consent is necessary. We must give Him our hearty cooperation.

"I will spew thee out of My mouth"

Warm water produces nausea and is administered as an emetic in case of poisoning. Also indifference and lack of conversion are repulsive to God, and those who persist in this condition will have to be dismissed from the presence of the Father.

Jesus sorrows over this lukewarmness and mediocrity. He expresses His fervent desire that the situation might change: "I would thou wert cold or hot."

"It would be more pleasing to the Lord if lukewarm professors of religion had never named His name. They are a continual weight to those who would be faithful followers of Jesus. They are a stumbling block to unbelievers."—1T 188.

But this need not be the condition of any of God's children.

The severity of the divine denunciation is intended to arouse us to a reformation of life, to a change so marked that it will reveal the profound and converting work of the grace of Christ.

Spiritual infatuation and self-justification

The substance of the message of the Faithful Witness is supported by this additional alarming revelation:

"Because thou sayest, I am rich, and increased with goods, and have need of nothing; and knowest not that thou art wretched, and miserable, and poor, and blind, and naked." Revelation 3:17.

The children of God who partake of the Laodicean spirit are represented as in a position of carnal security and in an attitude of smug self-righteousness. They are satisfied. They believe themselves to be in an exalted spiritual condition. But their situation is deplorable in the eyes of God. And they do not know it. They are deceived.

"The message to the Laodiceans is applicable to Seventh-day Adventists *who have had great light and have not walked in the light*. It is those who have made great profession, but have not kept in step with their Leader, that will be spewed out of His mouth unless they repent."—2SM 66.

The message shatters their security with the startling announcement of their true condition of spiritual blindness, poverty, and misery. Such infatuation is particularly serious because it places the victim who clings to it beyond the saving power of God. Recognition of our plight is an indispensable requisite for restoration by the divine Physician.

"They that are whole have no need of the physician, but they that are sick," said the Lord. And He added: "I came not to call the righteous, but sinners to repentance." Mark 2:17. The truth is, nevertheless, that "there is none righteous, no, not one." Romans 3:10; see also verse 23.

Who then are the "whole"? As used here the term designates the spiritually presumptuous, those who are filled with self-righteousness, like the Pharisee of the parable. These, with their present attitude, cannot be pardoned. They cannot be justified. Their prayers are ineffectual.

To these the counsel is, "Repent." Revelation 3:19. Repentance implies: (*a*) recognition of sin; (*b*) sorrow for sin; and (*c*) a desire to forsake it. But a heart full of self-righteousness—of what can it repent? And without repentance how can one obtain pardon and divine mercy?

There is nothing that makes the saving power of the gospel more inaccessible to sinners than this spiritual pride, this false front, this self-righteousness. It places them at the opposite pole from justification by faith, their only way of obtaining pardon and victory.

This sentiment of "I am rich" expresses the ultimate in self-righteousness, which the prophet Isaiah correctly describes as "filthy rags." Isaiah 64:6. He who partakes of this spirit may display abundant foliage of profession but have a life devoid of fruit, like the barren fig tree. With good reason Paul wished to escape this condition. His prayer was, "That I may win Christ, and be found in Him, not having mine own righteousness, which is of the law, but that which is through the faith of Christ, the righteousness which is of God by faith." Philippians 3:8, 9.

This message will benefit us if we volunteer our cooperation and sincere interest. Declares the pen of inspiration:

"I was shown that the testimony to the Laodiceans applies to God's people at the present time, and the reason it has not accomplished a greater work is because of the hardness of their hearts. But God has given the message time to do its work. The heart must be purified from sins which have so long shut out Jesus. This fearful message will do its work. When it was first presented, it led to close examination of heart. Sins were confessed, and the people of God were stirred everywhere. . . . It is designed to arouse the people of God, to discover to them their backslidings, and to lead to zealous repentance, that they may be favored with the presence of Jesus, and be fitted for the loud cry of the third angel."—1T 186.

An effective remedy

But the loving message of the Faithful Witness does more than merely denounce the sad spiritual condition of Laodicea. It does more than diagnose the sickness; it offers the remedy. Thus "the counsel of the True Witness is full of encouragement and comfort."—7BC 965.

"I counsel thee," says Jesus, "to buy of Me gold tried in the fire, that thou mayest be rich; and white raiment, that thou mayest be clothed, and that the shame of thy nakedness do not appear; and anoint thine eyes with eyesalve, that thou mayest see." Revelation 3:18.

The triple affliction of Laodicea—poverty, nakedness, blindness—is cured with the marvelous triple remedy of heaven: (a) gold tried in the fire, to make rich; (b) white raiment, to cover the nakedness; (c) eyesalve, to restore sight.

What is symbolized by these three?

"The gold here recommended as having been tried in the fire is faith and love. It makes the heart rich; for it has been purged until it is pure, and the more it is tested the more brilliant is its luster. The white raiment is purity of character, the righteousness of Christ imparted to the sinner. This is indeed a garment of heavenly texture, that can be bought only of Christ for a life of willing obedience. The eyesalve is that wisdom and grace which enables us to discern between the evil and the good, and to detect sin under any guise."—4T 88 (1TT 477, 478).

Faith and love

The faith and the love represented by the gold tried in the fire, are two important fruits of the Holy Spirit. Concerning their importance Ellen G. White writes:

"The gold mentioned by Christ, the True Witness, which all must have, has been shown me to be faith and love combined, and love takes the precedence of faith. Satan is constantly at work to remove these precious gifts from the hearts of God's people. All are engaged in playing the game of life. Satan is well aware that if he can remove love and faith, and supply their place with selfishness and unbelief, all the remaining precious traits will soon be skillfully removed by his deceitful hand, and the game will be lost."—2T 36, 37.

Love underlies true obedience to law. It is the supreme guiding principle of the converted, Christlike life. Without love there is no Christianity, because "he that loveth not knoweth not God; for God is love." 1 John 4:8.

Love radically transforms life. See 1 Corinthians 13. It eliminates conceit and selfishness and creates instead generosity, benevolence, and interest in the well-being of others.

Love cancels resentment, envy, and jealousy and replaces them with kindness, forbearance, and cordiality. It dispels contention and disloyal strife; it kills selfish ambition; it neutralizes hatred; it obliterates rancor and anger; it introduces peace, goodwill, and joy. It dispels fear and distrust.

Together with faith in Christ's pardon for sin, love is the best treatment for the ills of the spirit, the best solution for emotional problems, and withal a powerful medicine for healing many psychosomatic infirmities.

The only way to have love is to appropriate it from the blessed Source: Christ Jesus. Thus the apostle Paul counsels: "That Christ may dwell in your hearts by faith; that ye, being rooted and grounded in love." Ephesians 3:17. When Christ makes His triumphal entry into the heart and takes possession of the life ("I live; yet not I, but Christ liveth in me"), love becomes the supreme motivation: "The love of Christ constraineth us." Galatians 2:20; 2 Corinthians 5:14.

Faith, along with love, permits us to live constantly in the peaceful atmosphere of heaven. It establishes between our souls and God a link so indestructible that nothing or nobody can break it, except sin. It makes accessible to us the forgiveness of God and His power to live the victorious life. Faith puts at our disposal the fulfillment of all the promises of God. It is an active principle that manifests itself in the life by a voluntary obedience to the commandments of the Lord.

Justification by faith

The white raiment, which represents the righteousness of Christ applied to the life of the sinner, consists of a mantle of heavenly fabric, woven in the loom of heaven. This vesture can be obtained only by faith.

The problem of how to become righteous is as ancient as sin. Since the day in which our first parents violated the law of God and were made subject to eternal death, humanity has been seeking anxiously the way to acquire again justification, that is, a spiritual state of reconciliation with God. One of Job's friends expressed the question for all when he asked, "How then can man be justified with God?" Job 25:4.

Sin is the root of all human ills. It separates man from God

and plunges him into sorrow and desperation. A large proportion of neurotic patients who seek relief by consulting doctors
and psychiatrists are tormented with a sense of guilt.

Some time ago the writer was profoundly impressed, while
visiting some of the important cities of Latin America, to see
long files of men and women, young and old, waiting their turn
to kneel before the confessional. In some churches there were
as many as six long lines—souls seeking justification.

Man may seek righteousness by two methods. The first is by
his own efforts, hoping by compliance with law or by meritorious
works at last to gain favor with God. This is the most common
method. But it is un-Biblical and totally ineffectual. The other
method consists in recognizing one's own helplessness and in
exercising faith in the sacrifice of Christ on our behalf. This
is the only way to God.

Even the children of God can at times lose sight of one of
the most important truths of the Bible: that "by the deeds of the
law there shall no flesh be justified in His sight." Romans 3:20.

The Laodicean condition tends toward self-righteousness. A
person benumbed by it easily reaches the conclusion that, because of the knowledge of Bible truths, solidly established and
logically linked together, he has acquired spiritual excellence
which places him above other Christians. Such a person con-
tents himself with the thought that obedience to God's law will
gain for him divine favor and open for him the doors of heaven
as a right. He thus begins to commend himself, as did the
Pharisee in the parable: "I am rich, and increased with goods,
and have need of nothing." But the Lord replies to him:
"[Thou] knowest not that thou art wretched, and miserable, and
poor, and blind, and naked." And then He points out the
remedy: "I counsel thee to buy of Me . . . white raiment"—
that is, the only righteousness of value, the righteousness of
Christ.

"We are all as an unclean thing, and all our righteousnesses
are as filthy rags," says the prophet Isaiah. Not one thing can
man do to gain God's favor. The only merit which man can
claim resides in Christ, who is ready to cover the shame of our
nakedness with His pure mantle of righteousness.

Good works, as we will see later, enter the picture of our

salvation, but not as something we do *in order to be* justified, not as arguments to gain divine favor, or as credits toward the purchase price of heaven. Good works, obedience, appear as *an evidence of our faith,* as a demonstration of the power of God which works in us. But the only *right* to eternal life is the perfect righteousness of Christ which He grants to us unmerited on the basis of our faith.

"I will greatly rejoice in the Lord," declares again the gospel prophet, "my soul shall be joyful in my God; for He hath clothed me with the garments of salvation, He hath covered me with the robe of righteousness." Isaiah 61:10. Only when this lovely mantle—provided by the propitiatory death of Christ and His perfect life in our stead—covers human nakedness, can man appear perfect in the eyes of God. He is justified with the only effective righteousness, that of Christ.

But Christ offers us this marvelous white robe on two indispensable conditions:

1. The recognition of one's own sinfulness, weakness, and unworthiness, which leads to sincere repentance. That is why the message to Laodicea is a message of repentance. "Repent," says Christ. Put away your pride. Forsake your spiritual infatuation. Break your heart before the Lord and fall upon the Rock of your salvation.

2. The appropriation by faith of the righteousness of Christ, which He wants first to *impute* to us and afterward to *impart* to us.

"Therefore we conclude," says Paul, "that a man is justified by faith without the deeds of the law." Romans 3:28.

The pen of inspiration has explained in a short but majestic paragraph the true essence of justification by faith:

"What is justification by faith? It is the work of God in laying the glory of man in the dust, and doing for man that which it is not in his power to do for himself."—TM 456.

Two classes of righteousness

In another magnificent brief statement of Heaven's provision the servant of God says:

"The righteousness by which we are *justified* is *imputed;* the righteousness by which we are *sanctified* is *imparted.* The first is our *title* to heaven, the second is our *fitness* for heaven."—MYP 35.

In this most illuminating paragraph, the writer traces two distinct phases in the process of our salvation—two complementary aspects of the plan of redemption—which are in a certain sense successive, but at the same time simultaneous; two different operations of the same righteousness of Christ, which alone can satisfy the demands of divine justice and make saints of us.

Let us analyze in outline form these two phases:

A. *THE RIGHTEOUSNESS OF CHRIST BY WHICH WE ARE JUSTIFIED*

1. It is *imputed* to us, that is, credited, granted freely without our earning it.

2. It provides our *right* to heaven. It is the only merit we can claim.

3. *It justifies us,* that is, by it we are reckoned righteous in God's sight.

4. We receive it entirely *by faith,* and in free and unmerited form.

   —Ephesians 2:8, 9: "For by grace are ye *saved through faith;* and that not of yourselves: it is the gift of God: not of works, lest any man should boast."

   —Romans 3:24: "Being justified *freely* by His grace through the redemption that is in Christ Jesus."

   —Romans 5:1: "Therefore being justified *by faith,* we have peace with God through our Lord Jesus Christ."

5. Faith involves *repentance, confession,* and the *acceptance* of Christ as our Saviour. This means that we make a move toward God. We are saved under a law that if we ask, we receive the thing we ask for.

B. *THE RIGHTEOUSNESS OF CHRIST BY WHICH WE ARE SANCTIFIED*

1. It is *imparted* in a gradual, invisible process of Christian growth.

2. It provides our *fitness,* or preparation, for heaven.

3. It *sanctifies* us, or changes us into saints, transforming our characters.

4. It, also, is received *by means of faith.*

RIGHTEOUSNESS OF CHRIST

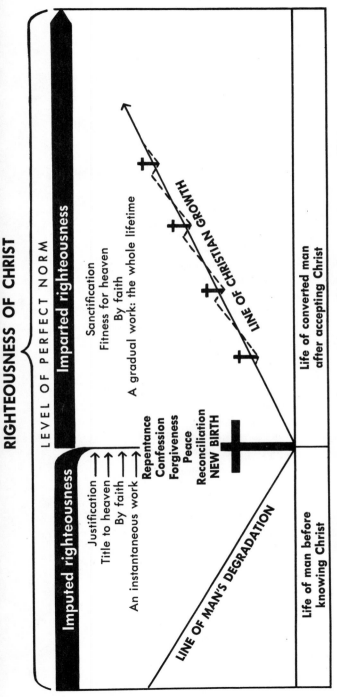

LEVEL OF PERFECT NORM

Imputed righteousness

Justification →
Title to heaven →
By faith →
An instantaneous work →

Repentance
Confession
Forgiveness
Peace
Reconciliation
NEW BIRTH

Imparted righteousness

Sanctification
Fitness for heaven
By faith
A gradual work: the whole lifetime

LINE OF MAN'S DEGRADATION

LINE OF CHRISTIAN GROWTH

Life of man before knowing Christ

Life of converted man after accepting Christ

The large cross represents the moment in which the sinner accepts Christ, repents, and confesses his sins for the first time. Right then Christ imputes to him His righteousness and forgives him. Thus, a new birth is produced and a new life of ascension toward perfection begins.

Nevertheless, in his progressive march, the converted man may fall. Every time this occurs, the experience of the imputed righteousness is repeated and the penitent is forgiven. So, man arises to continue his ascending march. This way, the process of imparted righteousness, which brings him always closer to the ideal, is combined with the experience of imputed righteousness, which reconciles him with God every time he falls into sin.

Imparted sanctification, or righteousness

The white raiment which the Faithful Witness counsels us to buy from Him represents not only justification, that is, the imputed righteousness of Christ, Heaven's provision for covering our moral nakedness and pardoning our sins. It represents also the following and complementary stage, sanctification, that is, imparted righteousness. This embraces habitual victory over sin, gradual transformation of character, Christian growth—upward progress in overcoming weaknesses and imperfections.

Whereas justification is an instant experience—because God pardons us and cleanses us the same moment we repent, confess the sin, and ask for pardon (1 John 1:7-9)—sanctification is a linear process that progresses throughout a lifetime.

It is certain that sanctification, continuing victory over sin, is an indispensable complement to justification, the pardon of God. One without the other would be illogical.

The peace made possible by pardon and reconciliation with God will be very brief if it is not accompanied by transformation of life which makes us hate sin and love righteousness. This new life enables us also to "bring forth therefore fruits meet for repentance." Matthew 3:8.

Justification is our right to heaven. The thief on the cross, without having had opportunity to live any length of time after the forgiveness of his sins, will be saved. The application of Christ's imputed righteousness presented him perfect and entire in the sight of heaven. Likewise, God does not see the spiritual wretchedness of the penitent prodigal today, nor the shame of his nakedness; but the precious robe with which Christ has covered him. He does not see the record of his sin, but the perfection of the life of Christ, who freely forgave him the moment he repented.

But the right, or *title,* to heaven is not enough. It is necessary for us to have a *fitness* to live there. We must have a *preparation.* Suppose we should win a contest in which some airline would grant us free passage to a distant and very cold country. We would hold the ticket (the *title*) for the trip, but we would still find it necessary to provide the proper clothing for our stay. In the same way the Lord expects us to prepare Christlike characters for heaven, to exercise voluntary obedience to His precepts, to walk in the light He causes to shine on our pathway, to advance each day one step nearer perfection. And thus we can be always perfect with respect to our age in Christ, fulfilling the command of Jesus: "Be ye therefore perfect, even as your Father which is in heaven is perfect." Matthew 5:48.

THE SECRET OF VICTORY

In order to experience these results, we must depend completely on Christ. The basis of both imputed and imparted righteousness is faith. But faith is an active principle which causes us to renounce self and surrender ourselves daily and entirely to the Lord so that He may live in us.

The differential between the perfection represented by our "age" in Christ—which we have gained by the grace of God— and the perfection which is the final goal, the Lord Jesus makes up each moment with His imputed righteousness. He imputes, or attributes, to us not only the merits of His blood—that which delivers us from death—but also the merits of His perfect life.

This is possible because Christ complied with the law, not only in His life but also on the cross. Not only did He pay the penalty demanded from each of us, but He also fulfills the law by living it in us and by giving us the victory.

Sanctification is God's work in our lives. To the woman taken in adultery, after He had pardoned her, Christ said, "Go, and sin no more." John 8:11. The apostle Peter echoes God's plan for man when he says: "The One who called you is holy; like Him, be holy in all your behavior." 1 Peter 1:15, N.E.B.

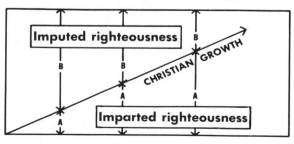

LEVEL OF PERFECT NORM

Imputed righteousness

CHRISTIAN GROWTH

Imparted righteousness

INITIAL LEVEL OF SINNER'S LIFE

Christ's imputed righteousness not only brings about pardon of sin on the virtue of Jesus' DEATH but applies the merits of Christ's perfect LIFE to the sinner. The difference between imparted righteousness Ⓐ and the level of the perfect norm (difference Ⓑ that implies a deficiency in the life of man), is supplied by Christ by His imputed righteousness.

Every Christian knows from experience, however, that along the ascending pathway toward sanctification accidents and relapses take place. The old weaknesses reassert themselves. It is because of this that the Word assures us of pardon through the mediation of Christ. Even though John says, "These things write I unto you, that ye sin not," he completes the sentence with the great divine promise: "And if any man sin, we have an advocate with the Father, Jesus Christ the righteous." 1 John 2:1. "And the blood of Jesus Christ His Son cleanseth us from all sin." 1 John 1:7.

"When it is in the heart to obey God, when efforts are put forth to this end, Jesus accepts this disposition and effort as man's best service, and He makes up for the deficiency with His own divine merit."—1SM 382.

Thus imputed righteousness and imparted righteousness are integrated, mutually complementing each other. They are essentially two aspects of the same operation.

"Higher than the highest human thought can reach is God's ideal for His children. Godliness—godlikeness—is the goal to be reached. Before the student there is opened a path of continual progress. He has an object to achieve, a standard to attain, that includes everything good, and pure, and noble."—Ed 18.

The white raiment of Revelation is also mentioned by Jesus in the parable of the wedding feast. Matthew 22:11-13. A special garment was provided for the feast. The one who refused to put it on was expelled. Anyone who refuses to divest himself of his own soiled character and obtain the perfect character of Christ will not be able to take part in the wedding supper of the Lamb.

"By the wedding garment in the parable is represented the pure, spotless character which Christ's true followers will possess. . . . It is the righteousness of Christ, His own unblemished character, that through faith is imparted to all who receive Him as their personal Saviour."—COL 310.

A message of reformation

The message to Laodicea is therefore not only a call to repentance and justification by faith; it is also a divine invitation to possess the character of Christ, His righteousness, His holiness. It is a message of reformation.

The process of sanctification requires time and perseverance. Holiness is not the work of a moment; it is the harvest of a lifetime. But although one is subjected to a trying battle with the powers of evil, this battle begins with the guarantee of triumph:

"Christ has given us no assurance that to attain perfection of character is an easy matter. A noble, all-round character is not inherited. It does not come to us by accident. A noble character is earned by individual effort through the merits and grace of Christ. . . . It is formed by hard, stern battle with self. Conflict after conflict must be waged against hereditary tendencies. We shall have to criticize ourselves closely, and allow not one unfavorable trait to remain uncorrected."—COL 331.

But in spite of the difficulties that beset us in perfecting character, the Bible assures us that the goal can be reached. God never asks for impossibilities. His commands are enablings.

"Let no one say, I cannot remedy my defects of character. If you come to this decision, you will certainly fail of obtaining everlasting life. The impossibility lies in your own will. If you will not, then you cannot overcome. The real difficulty arises from the corruption of an unsanctified heart, and an unwillingness to submit to the control of God."—Ibid.

We must learn how to renounce self and give ourselves completely to Christ, to "Him that is able to keep you from falling, and to present you faultless before the presence of His glory." Jude 24. We must learn now to depend every moment on Him who said, "Without Me ye can do nothing" (John 15:5), and, "All power is given unto Me in heaven and in earth." Matthew 28:18. Then, with Paul, we can say, "I can do all things through Christ which strengtheneth me." Philippians 4:13. That which is impossible because of the weakness of the flesh, God makes possible through Christ. Romans 8:3, 4. With the apostle we can exclaim: "Now thanks be unto God, which always causeth us to triumph in Christ." 2 Corinthians 2:14.

The basis of this whole experience of triumph is faith. "This is the victory that overcometh the world," says John, "even our faith." 1 John 5:4. Faith is the strong wheel which causes us to ascend the hill of sanctification on the road to the heights of victory. But the hub of this wheel is Christ. Faith is not the

The wheel of faith carries us along the
road of sanctification to the heights of
victory.
But the hub of the wheel is Christ. Christ
is the Saviour.

Saviour. Christ is the Saviour. In Him our hopes and our
strength are centered.

It is faith that leads us to surrender. Then will be produced
a great miracle: Christ triumphs in us and for us.

"When the soul surrenders itself to Christ, a new power takes
possession of the new heart. A change is wrought which man can
never accomplish for himself. It is a supernatural work, bringing a
supernatural element into human nature. The soul that is yielded
to Christ becomes His own fortress, which He holds in a revolted
world. . . . A soul thus kept in possession by the heavenly agencies
is impregnable to the assaults of Satan."—DA 324.

CONCLUSION

The message of the Faithful Witness is, then, not only a
message of justification and pardon, a call not only to repentance,
but also a call to total conversion, sanctification, and reformation
of life. This is the true reformation which must be effected in
the ranks of God's people. It is this reformation which will hasten
the pouring out of God's power in the latter rain, the proclamation of the everlasting gospel, and the sealing. This is the reformation of life which each one of us must have in order to pass
triumphantly through the time of trouble and welcome the Lord
with great joy. This is the experience which will permit us
to be prepared to live with God and with Christ throughout
eternity.

CHAPTER 2

THE SEALING

Synthesis—Description of the event—What is the seal of God?—When the sealing occurs: time and duration—Conditions in order to be sealed.

SYNTHESIS

THE SEALING, a spiritual process invisible to human eyes, is now under way and will be finished soon, at the close of probation. As it relates to individuals, the sealing work begins for each Christian on the day of his conversion, and it ends for him at the close of probation, whether this be at his death or at the end of the investigative judgment. This work, accomplished by the angels of God and the Holy Spirit, consists of writing the principles of the divine law—including the fourth commandment—in the life of every submissive soul.

The sealing accomplishes the following objectives:

1. It fixes in the life the principles of God's law.

2. It makes faithful Sabbath observance possible for those who are sealed as they meet apostasy and fierce persecution.

3. It prepares them to pass unharmed through the time of trouble and to live above sin while they are without a Mediator.

4. It preserves them from the final destruction.

DESCRIPTION OF THE EVENT

"And after these things I saw four angels standing on the four corners of the earth, holding the four winds of the earth, that the wind should not blow on the earth, nor on the sea, nor on any tree. And I saw another angel ascending from the east, having the seal of the living God: and he cried with a loud voice to the

49

four angels, to whom it was given to hurt the earth and the sea, saying, Hurt not the earth, neither the sea, nor the trees, till we have sealed the servants of our God in their foreheads. And I heard the number of them which were sealed: and there were sealed an hundred and forty and four thousand of all the tribes of the children of Israel." Revelation 7:1-4.

"Just as soon as the people of God are sealed in their foreheads —it is not any seal or mark that can be seen, but a settling into the truth, both intellectually and spiritually, so they cannot be moved —just as soon as God's people are sealed and prepared for the shaking, it will come. Indeed, it has begun already; the judgments of God are now upon the land, to give us warning, that we may know what is coming."—4BC 1161.

"While one class, by accepting the sign of submission to earthly powers, receive the mark of the beast, the other, choosing the token of allegiance to divine authority, receive the seal of God."—GC 605.

"I was pointed down to the time when the third angel's message was closing. The power of God had rested upon His people; they had accomplished their work and were prepared for the trying hour before them. They had received the latter rain, or refreshing from the presence of the Lord, and the living testimony had been revived. The last great warning had sounded everywhere, and it had stirred up and enraged the inhabitants of the earth who would not receive the message.

"I saw angels hurrying to and fro in heaven. An angel with a writer's inkhorn by his side returned from the earth and reported to Jesus that his work was done, and the saints were numbered and sealed. Then I saw Jesus, who had been ministering before the ark containing the Ten Commandments, throw down the censer. He raised His hands, and with a loud voice said, 'It is done.' "—EW 279.

"While Satan was urging his accusations and seeking to destroy this company, holy angels, unseen, were passing to and fro, placing upon them the seal of the living God. These are they that stand upon Mount Zion with the Lamb, having the Father's name written in their foreheads."—5T 475, 476 (2TT 179).

"This sealing of the servants of God is the same that was shown to Ezekiel in vision. John also had been a witness of this most startling revelation. He saw the sea and the waves roaring, and men's hearts failing them for fear. He beheld the earth moved, and the mountains carried into the midst of the sea (which is literally taking place), the water thereof roaring and troubled, and the mountains shaking with the swelling thereof. He was shown plagues, pestilence, famine, and death performing their terrible mission."—TM 445, 446.

"The mighty angel is seen ascending from the east (or sunrising). This mightiest of angels has in his hand the seal of the living God, or of Him who alone can give life, who can inscribe upon the foreheads the mark or inscription, to whom shall be granted immortality, eternal life."—TM 444, 445.

"The Lord is doing His work. All heaven is astir. The Judge of all the earth is soon to arise and vindicate His insulted authority. The mark of deliverance will be set upon the men who keep God's commandments, who revere His law, and who refuse the mark of the beast or of his image."—5T 451, 452 (2TT 151).

"Satan is now using every device in this sealing time to keep the minds of God's people from the present truth and to cause them to waver. I saw a covering that God was drawing over His people to protect them in the time of trouble; and every soul that was decided on the truth and was pure in heart was to be covered with the covering of the Almighty."—EW 43.

WHAT IS THE SEAL OF GOD?

Two things may be called a "seal": (1) The *instrument* that is used for stamping a mark; and (2) the *mark* itself.

When we refer to the seal of God, the sealing *instrument* is the law of God as a whole, and the Sabbath, or the fourth commandment, in a more specific sense, because it is the commandment that bears the inscription of the Lawgiver's name, title, and authority. The law and the Sabbath reflect the perfection of God and the transforming work of His Spirit.

On the other hand, the seal of God, interpreted as the *mark* itself, or as the result of applying the instrument to a document, is a character like that of Christ, the divine perfection reflected in the life of the child of God. The sealing is the definite "settling" of a human being into the truth, the permanent fixing of the law in his life.

Moreover, just as a seal can be applied only to an authentic document, so also the seal of God can be applied only to the life of a real Christian, a consecrated life, one washed with the blood of Christ and renewed in holiness according to the standards of God's law.

"Ye were sealed with that Holy Spirit of promise." Ephesians 1:13. "And grieve not the Holy Spirit of God, whereby ye are sealed unto the day of redemption." Ephesians 4:30.

"What is the seal of the living God, which is placed in the foreheads of His people? It is a mark which angels, but not human eyes, can read; for the destroying angel must see this mark of redemption."—4BC 1161.

"The angel with the writer's inkhorn is to place a mark upon the foreheads of all who are separated from sin and sinners, and the destroying angel follows this angel."—4BC 1161.

"The fourth commandment is the only one of all the ten in which are found both the name and the title of the Lawgiver. It is the only one that shows by whose authority the law is given. Thus it contains the seal of God, affixed to His law as evidence of its authenticity and binding force."—PP 307.

"While living under and proclaiming the most solemn message ever borne to mortals, presenting the law of God as a test of character and as the seal of the living God, they [certain professed Seventh-day Adventists living in flagrant sin] are transgressing its holy precepts."—2T 468.

"The sign, or seal, of God is revealed in the observance of the seventh-day Sabbath, the Lord's memorial of creation. 'The Lord spake unto Moses, saying, Speak thou also unto the children of Israel, saying, Verily My Sabbaths ye shall keep: for it is a sign between Me and you throughout your generations; that ye may know that I am the Lord that doth sanctify you.' Exodus 31:12, 13. Here the Sabbath is clearly designated as a sign between God and His people."—8T 117 (3TT 232).

WHEN THE SEALING OCCURS: TIME AND DURATION

"The sealing time is very short, and will soon be over. Now is the time, while the four angels are holding the four winds, to make our calling and election sure."—EW 58.

"If such scenes as this are to come, such tremendous judgments on a guilty world, where will be the refuge for God's people? How will they be sheltered until the indignation be overpast? John sees the elements of nature—earthquake, tempest, and political strife—represented as being held by four angels. These winds are under control until God gives the word to let them go. There is the safety of God's church. The angels of God do His bidding, holding back the winds of the earth, that the winds should not blow on the earth, nor on the sea, nor on any tree, until the servants of God should be sealed in their foreheads. The mighty angel is seen ascending from the east (or sunrising). This mightiest of angels has in his hand the seal of the living God, or of Him who alone can give life, who can inscribe upon the foreheads the mark or inscription, to whom shall be granted immortality, eternal life. It is the voice of this highest angel that had authority to command the four angels to keep in check the four winds until this work was performed, and until he should give the summons to let them loose."—TM 444, 445.

"When this time of trouble comes, every case is decided; there is no longer probation, no longer mercy for the impenitent. The seal of the living God is upon His people."—5T 213 (2TT 67).

CONDITIONS IN ORDER TO BE SEALED

Only those who have been sealed will be able to pass successfully through the time of trouble and meet the Lord in peace.

"Many hear the invitation of mercy, are tested and proved; but few are sealed with the seal of the living God. Few will humble themselves as a little child, that they may enter the kingdom of heaven."—5T 50.

"Now is the time to prepare. The seal of God will never be placed upon the forehead of an impure man or woman. It will never be placed upon the forehead of the ambitious, world-loving man or woman. It will never be placed upon the forehead of men or women of false tongues or deceitful hearts. All who receive the seal must be without spot before God—candidates for heaven."—5T 216.

"Jesus is in His holy temple and will now accept our sacrifices, our prayers, and our confessions of faults and sins and will pardon all the transgressions of Israel, that they may be blotted out before He leaves the sanctuary. When Jesus leaves the sanctuary, then they who are holy and righteous will be holy and righteous still; for all their sins will then be blotted out, and they will be sealed with the seal of the living God. But those that are unjust and filthy will be unjust and filthy still."—EW 48.

"Those who receive the seal of the living God and are protected in the time of trouble must reflect the image of Jesus fully."—EW 71.

"No sin can be tolerated in those who shall walk with Christ in white. The filthy garments are to be removed, and Christ's robe of righteousness is to be placed upon us. By repentance and faith we are enabled to render obedience to all the commandments of God, and are found without blame before Him. Those who shall meet

the approval of God are now afflicting their souls, confessing their sins, and earnestly pleading for pardon through Jesus their Advocate."
—5T 472 (2TT 175).

"Not one of us will ever receive the seal of God while our characters have one spot or stain upon them. It is left with us to remedy the defects in our characters, to cleanse the soul temple of every defilement. Then the latter rain will fall upon us as the early rain fell upon the disciples on the Day of Pentecost."—5T 214 (2TT 69).

"I saw that those who of late have embraced the truth would have to know what it is to suffer for Christ's sake, that they would have trials to pass through that would be keen and cutting, in order that they may be purified and fitted through suffering to receive the seal of the living God, pass through the time of trouble, see the King in His beauty, and dwell in the presence of God and of pure, holy angels. . . .

"But now time is almost finished, and what we have been years learning, they will have to learn in a few months. They will also have much to unlearn and much to learn again."—EW 67.

"Those that overcome the world, the flesh, and the devil, will be the favored ones who shall receive the seal of the living God. Those whose hands are not clean, whose hearts are not pure, will not have the seal of the living God. Those who are planning sin and acting it will be passed by. Only those who, in their attitude before God, are filling the position of those who are repenting and confessing their sins in the great antitypical day of atonement, will be recognized and marked as worthy of God's protection."—TM 445.

CHAPTER 3

THE LATTER RAIN

Synthesis—Description—Purpose—Importance and neces-
sity—Promises and willingness of God—Conditions—Re-
sults of the latter rain.

SYNTHESIS

THE HOLY SPIRIT excels every other gift God can bestow upon an individual or the church. In fact, His reception brings all other spiritual blessings in His train.

He stands as the Third Person of the Godhead, and comes to men as the personal representative of God and of Christ. By divine power He softens hearts and points out matters that need attention. Without Him not a single soul would be converted.

Some of the functions of the Holy Spirit can be listed as follows:

1. To convince of sin, of justice, and of judgment, producing repentance in the heart. John 16:8.

2. To direct the mind in the study of the Word of God, guiding it into all truth. John 14:26; 16:13.

3. To bring to remembrance in moments of necessity or emergency truths or Bible passages already studied. John 14:26; Mark 13:11.

4. To intercede for us before the Father when we pray, interpreting and perfecting our supplications. Romans 8:26.

5. To give us proof or internal assurance that we are children of God. Romans 8:16.

6. To enable the children of God to proclaim the gospel with success and with power. Acts 1:8.

The Holy Spirit has, of course, been working in man's behalf

55

throughout the ages, but the Lord records promises in His Word of an abundant and extraordinary outpouring or effusion of this power to fit the church for doing a special work in special times.

In this sense the "early rain," first fulfillment of the prophetic promise, gave the apostles ability to accomplish their prodigious work. The "latter rain," which is to occur in our days, will enable the church to finish the great gospel task according to plan.

Realizing the transcending importance of the latter rain to the church, we should earnestly pray for it.

Although we have already seen here and there isolated showers, the latter rain in marvelous abundance will descend only when the major part of the church—ministers and laity—experience the necessary revival and reformation and comply with the required conditions.

DESCRIPTION

"Be glad then, ye children of Zion, and rejoice in the Lord your God: for He hath given you the former rain moderately, and He will cause to come down for you the rain, the former rain, and the latter rain in the first month." Joel 2:23.

"And it shall come to pass afterward, that I will pour out My Spirit upon all flesh; and your sons and your daughters shall prophesy, your old men shall dream dreams, your young men shall see visions: and also upon the servants and upon the hand-maids in those days will I pour out My Spirit. And I will show wonders in the heavens and in the earth, blood, and fire, and pillars of smoke. The sun shall be turned into darkness, and the moon into blood, before the great and the terrible day of the Lord come." Verses 28-31.

This promise is repeated in Acts 2:17-20.

"Then shall we know, if we follow on to know the Lord: His going forth is prepared as the morning; and He shall come unto us as the rain, as the latter and former rain unto the earth." Hosea 6:3.

"Under the figure of the early and the latter rain, that falls in Eastern lands at seedtime and harvest, the Hebrew prophets foretold the bestowal of spiritual grace in extraordinary measure upon God's church. The outpouring of the Spirit in the days of the apostles was the beginning of the early, or former, rain, and glorious was the result. To the end of time the presence of the Spirit is to abide with the true church."—AA 54, 55.

PURPOSE

"At that time the 'latter rain,' or refreshing from the presence of the Lord, will come, to give power to the loud voice of the third angel, and prepare the saints to stand in the period when the seven last plagues shall be poured out."—EW 86.

"It is the latter rain which revives and strengthens them to pass through the time of trouble. Their faces will shine with the glory of that light which attends the third angel."—7BC 984.

"The work will be similar to that of the Day of Pentecost. As the 'former rain' was given, in the outpouring of the Holy Spirit at the opening of the gospel, to cause the upspringing of the precious seed, so the 'latter rain' will be given at its close for the ripening of the harvest."—GC 611.

IMPORTANCE AND NECESSITY

"This promised blessing, claimed by faith, brings all other blessings in its train. It is given according to the riches of the grace of Christ, and He is ready to supply every soul according to the capacity to receive."—GW 285.

Christian virtues and blessings are the fruit of the Spirit. Galatians 5:22, 23.

"At no point in our experience can we dispense with the assistance of that which enables us to make the first start. The blessings received under the former rain are needful to us to the end. Yet these alone will not suffice. While we cherish the blessing of the early rain, we must not, on the other hand, lose sight of the fact that without the latter rain, to fill out the ears and ripen the grain, the harvest will not be ready for the sickle, and the labor of the sower will have been in vain. Divine grace is needed at the beginning, divine grace at every step of advance, and divine grace alone can complete the work. There is no place for us to rest in a careless attitude. We must never forget the warnings of Christ, 'Watch unto prayer,' 'Watch, . . . and pray always.' A connection with the divine agency every moment is essential to our progress. We may have had a measure of the Spirit of God, but by prayer and faith we are continually to seek more of the Spirit. It will never do to cease our efforts. If we do not progress, if we do not place ourselves in an attitude to receive both the former and the latter rain, we shall lose our souls, and the responsibility will lie at our own door."—TM 507, 508.

PROMISES AND WILLINGNESS OF GOD

"If ye then, being evil, know how to give good gifts unto your children: how much more shall your heavenly Father give the Holy Spirit to them that ask Him?" Luke 11:13.

"It is not because of any restriction on the part of God that the riches of His grace do not flow earthward to men. . . . If all were willing, all would be filled with the Spirit. . . . The Lord is more willing to give the Holy Spirit to those who serve Him than parents are to give good gifts to their children. For the daily baptism of the Spirit every worker should offer his petition to God."—AA 50.

"The descent of the Holy Spirit upon the church is looked forward to as in the future; but it is the privilege of the church to have it now. Seek for it, pray for it, believe for it. We must have it, and Heaven is waiting to bestow it."—Ev 701.

"At this very hour His Spirit and His grace are for all who need them and will take Him at His word."—8T 20 (ChS 250).

The promises of God are for us. The time is now. The Lord is anxious to fulfill the promise. Why, then, does the latter rain seem to be delayed?

CONDITIONS

Because, as happens with each promise of God, fulfillment is subject to conditions which must be met. Notice the italicized words in the following paragraphs:

"Christ has promised the gift of the Holy Spirit to His church, and the promise belongs to us as much as to the first disciples. But like every other promise, *it is given on conditions*."—DA 672.

"This promised blessing, claimed by faith, brings all other blessings in its train. It is given according to the riches of the grace of Christ, and He is ready to supply every soul *according to the capacity to receive*."—Ibid.

"The Spirit works upon man's heart, *according to his desire and consent* implanting in him a new nature."—COL 411.

"Before the final visitation of God's judgments upon the earth there will be among the people of the Lord such *a revival of primitive godliness* as has not been witnessed since apostolic times. The Spirit and power of God will be poured out upon His children."—GC 464.

"Unless we are daily advancing in the exemplification of the active Christian virtues, we shall not recognize the manifestations of the Holy Spirit in the latter rain. It may be falling on hearts all around us, but we shall not discern or receive it. . . .

"If we do not place ourselves *in an attitude to receive both the former and the latter rain,* we shall lose our souls, and the responsibility will lie at our own door."—TM 507, 508.

And we pass now to an enumeration of some of the conditions:

1. To feel the need of the Spirit and to pray for His presence

"If all were willing, all would be filled with the Spirit. Wherever the need of the Holy Spirit is a matter little thought of, there is seen spiritual drought, spiritual darkness, spiritual declension and death. Whenever minor matters occupy the attention, the divine power which is necessary for the growth and prosperity of the church, and which would bring all other blessings in its train, is lacking, though offered in infinite plenitude.

"Since this is the means by which we are to receive power, why do we not hunger and thirst for the gift of the Spirit? Why do we not talk of it, pray for it, and preach concerning it? The Lord is more willing to give the Holy Spirit to those who serve Him than parents are to give good gifts to their children. For the daily baptism of the Spirit every worker should offer his petition to God."—AA 50.

"The Holy Spirit will come to all who are begging for the bread of life to give to their neighbors."—6T 90 (ChS 252).

"The great outpouring of the Spirit of God, which lightens the whole earth with His glory, will not come until we have an enlightened people, that know by experience what it means to be laborers together with God. When we have entire, wholehearted consecration to the service of Christ, God will recognize the fact by an outpouring of His Spirit without measure; but this will not be while the largest portion of the church are not laborers together with God."—ChS 253.

"The convocations of the church, as in camp meetings, the assemblies of the home church, and all occasions where there is personal labor for souls, are God's appointed opportunities for giving the early and the latter rain. . . .

"It is not an immutable law that all who attend general gatherings or local meetings shall receive large supplies from heaven. The circumstances may seem to be favorable for a rich outpouring of the showers of grace. But God Himself must command the rain to fall. Therefore we should not be remiss in supplication. We are not to trust to the ordinary working of providence. We must pray that God will unseal the fountain of the water of life. And we must ourselves receive of the living water. Let us, with contrite hearts, pray most earnestly that now, in the time of the latter rain, the showers of grace may fall upon us. At every meeting we attend our prayers should ascend, that at this very time God will impart warmth and moisture to our souls."—TM 508, 509.

"As you pray, believe, trust in God. It is the time of the latter rain, when the Lord will give largely of His Spirit. Be fervent in prayer, and watch in the Spirit."—TM 512.

2. To experience first the early rain

This implies complete confession and pardon of sin, cleansing from every defilement, fervent prayer, and the consecration of self to God. In a word: constant growth in the Christian graces, improving present opportunities.

"Many have in a great measure *failed to receive the former rain.* They have not obtained all the benefits that God has thus provided for them. They expect that the lack will be supplied by the latter rain. When the richest abundance of grace shall be bestowed, they intend to open their hearts to receive it. They are making a terrible mistake. The work that God has begun in the human heart in giving His light and knowledge must be continually going forward. Every individual must realize his own necessity. *The heart must be emptied of every defilement and cleansed for the indwelling of the Spirit.* It was by the *confession and forsaking of sin,* by *earnest prayer and consecration* of themselves to God, that the early disciples prepared for the outpouring of the Holy Spirit on the Day of Pentecost. The same work, only in greater degree, must be done now. Then the human agent had only to ask for the blessing, and wait for the Lord to perfect the work concerning him. It is God who began the work, and He will finish His work, making man complete in Jesus Christ. But *there must be no neglect of the grace represented by the former rain. Only those who are living up to the light they have will receive greater light.* Unless we are daily advancing in the exemplification of the active Christian virtues, we shall not recognize the manifestations of the Holy Spirit in the latter rain. It may be falling on hearts all around us, but we shall not discern or receive it."—TM 507.

"The religion of Christ means *more than the forgiveness of sin;* it means *taking away our sins,* and filling the vacuum with the graces of the Holy Spirit."—COL 419, 420.

"We may be sure that when the Holy Spirit is poured out *those who did not receive and appreciate the early rain will not see or understand the value of the latter rain.*"—TM 399.

"There are some who, instead of wisely improving present opportunities, are idly waiting for some special season of spiritual refreshing by which their ability to enlighten others will be greatly increased. *They neglect present duties and privileges, and allow their light to burn dim,* while they look forward to a time when, without any effort on their part, they will be made the recipients of special blessing, by which they will be transformed and fitted for service."—AA 54.

"Today you are to have your vessel purified that it may be ready for the heavenly dew, ready for the showers of the latter rain; for the latter rain will come, and the blessing of God will fill *every soul that is purified* from every defilement."—Ev 702.

"We must not wait for the latter rain. It is coming upon all who will recognize and appropriate the dew and showers of grace that fall upon us. When we gather up the fragments of light, when we appreciate the sure mercies of God, who loves to have us trust Him, then every promise will be fulfilled. [Isaiah 61:11 quoted.] The whole earth is to be filled with the glory of God."—7BC 984.

3. *To be willingly used and guided by the Spirit*

"Christ has promised the gift of the Holy Spirit to His church, and the promise belongs to us as much as to the first disciples. But like every other promise, it is given on conditions. There are many who believe and profess to claim the Lord's promise; they talk *about* Christ and *about* the Holy Spirit, yet receive no benefit. *They do not surrender the soul to be guided and controlled by the divine agencies. We cannot use the Holy Spirit. The Spirit is to use us.* Through the Spirit God works in His people 'to will and to do of His good pleasure.' Phil. 2:13. But many will not submit to this. They want to manage themselves. This is why they do not receive the heavenly gift. Only to those who wait humbly upon God, who watch for His guidance and grace, is the Spirit given."—DA 672.

4. *To eliminate dissensions and misunderstandings*

"Before the Day of Pentecost they met together, and put away all differences. They were of one accord."—DA 827.

"When the Day of Pentecost was fully come, they were all with one accord." Acts 2:1.

"Let Christians put away their dissensions, and give themselves to God for the saving of the lost. Let them in faith ask for the blessing, and it will come."—DA 827.

5. To surrender self

"He longs to pour upon us His Holy Spirit in rich measure, and He bids us clear the way by self-renunciation. *When self is surrendered to God,* our eyes will be opened to see the stumbling stones which our un-Christlikeness has placed in the way of others. All these God bids us remove. He says: 'Confess your faults one to another, and pray one for another, that ye may be healed.' James 5:16."—6T 43 (2TT 382).

"When one is *fully emptied of self,* when every false god is cast out of the soul, *the vacuum is filled by the inflowing of the Spirit of Christ.*"—GW 287.

"The time demands greater efficiency and deeper consecration. I cry to God, Raise up and send forth messengers filled with a sense of their responsibility, men in whose hearts *self-idolatry,* which lies at the foundation of all sin, *has been crucified;* who are willing to consecrate themselves without reserve to God's service; whose souls are alive to the sacredness of the work and the responsibility of their calling; who are determined not to bring to God a maimed sacrifice, which cost them neither effort nor prayer."—GW 114.

"No man can empty himself of self. *We can only consent for Christ to accomplish the work.* Then the language of the soul will be, Lord, take my heart; for I cannot give it. It is Thy property. Keep it pure, for I cannot keep it for Thee. Save me in spite of myself, my weak, un-Christlike self. Mold me, fashion me, raise me into a pure and holy atmosphere, where the rich current of Thy love can flow through my soul.

"It is not only at the beginning of the Christian life that this renunciation of self is to be made. At every advance step heavenward it is to be renewed."—COL 159, 160.

"There is *nothing so offensive to God or so dangerous* to the human soul *as pride and self-sufficiency.* Of all sins it is the most hopeless, the most incurable."—COL 154.

"There is no limit to the usefulness of the one who, *putting self aside,* makes room for the working of the Holy Spirit upon his heart, and lives a life wholly consecrated to God."—ChS 254.

"The minister for God should in an eminent degree possess humility. Those who have the *deepest experience in the things of God are the farthest removed from pride and self-exaltation.* Because they have an exalted conception of the glory of God, they feel that the lowest place in His service is too honorable for them."—GW 142.

RESULTS OF THE LATTER RAIN

"As the members of the body of Christ approach the period of their last conflict, 'the time of Jacob's trouble,' they will grow up into Christ, and will partake largely of His Spirit. As the third message swells to a loud cry, and as great power and glory attend the closing work, the faithful people of God will partake of that glory. It is the latter rain which revives and strengthens them to pass through the time of trouble. Their faces will shine with the glory of that light which attends the third angel."—7BC 984.

"I heard those clothed with the armor speak forth the truth with great power. It had effect. Many had been bound; some wives by their husbands, and some children by their parents. The honest who had been prevented from hearing the truth now eagerly laid hold upon it. All fear of their relatives was gone, and the truth alone was exalted to them. They had been hungering and thirsting for truth; it was dearer and more precious than life. I asked what had made this great change. An angel answered, 'It is the latter rain, the refreshing from the presence of the Lord, the loud cry of the third angel.' "—EW 271.

"When the final warning shall be given, it will arrest the attention of these leading men [men in national affairs] through whom the Lord is now working, and some of them will accept it, and will stand with the people of God through the time of trouble.

"The angel who unites in the proclamation of the third angel's message is to lighten the whole earth with his glory. A work of worldwide extent and unwonted power is here foretold. The advent movement of 1840-44 was a glorious manifestation of the power of God; the first angel's message was carried to every missionary station in the world, and in some countries there was the greatest religious interest which has been witnessed in any land since the Reformation of the sixteenth century; but these are to be exceeded by the mighty movement under the last warning of the third angel.

"The work will be similar to that of the Day of Pentecost. As the 'former rain' was given, in the outpouring of the Holy Spirit at the opening of the gospel, to cause the upspringing of the precious seed, so the 'latter rain' will be given at its close for the ripening of the harvest. . . .

"The great work of the gospel is not to close with less manifestation of the power of God than marked its opening. The prophecies which were fulfilled in the outpouring of the former rain at the opening of the gospel are again to be fulfilled in the latter rain at its close. Here are 'the times of refreshing' to which the apostle Peter looked forward when he said: 'Repent ye therefore, and be converted, that your sins may be blotted out, when the times of refreshing shall come from the presence of the Lord; and He shall send Jesus.' Acts 3:19, 20.

"Servants of God, with their faces lighted up and shining with holy consecration, will hasten from place to place to proclaim the message from heaven. By thousands of voices, all over the earth, the warning will be given. Miracles will be wrought, the sick will be healed, and signs and wonders will follow the believers."—GC 611, 612.

"The outpouring of the Spirit in apostolic days was the 'former rain,' and glorious was the result. But the 'latter rain' will be more abundant."—DA 827.

"These scenes are to be repeated, and with greater power. The outpouring of the Holy Spirit on the Day of Pentecost was the former rain, but the latter rain will be more abundant."—COL 121.

CHAPTER 4

THE SHAKING

Synthesis—Description of the process—Causes—The time—
Directions on how to avoid falling—Church will not fall;
sinners will be sifted out.

SYNTHESIS

THE INSPIRED PROPHET speaks symbolically of a shaking of God's people: "For, lo, I will command, and I will sift the house of Israel among all nations, like as corn is sifted in a sieve, yet shall not the least grain fall upon the earth." Amos 9:9.

And in a critical hour the Lord Jesus told Peter: "Simon, Simon, behold, Satan hath desired to have you, that he may sift you as wheat: but I have prayed for thee, that thy faith fail not." Luke 22:31, 32.

Every child of God individually, and the church as a whole, will undergo a special trial of faith. This test is called the "shaking" or "sifting." It has happened in times past and will be repeated near the end in a specific way. The enemy, knowing that he has but a short time, will work with increasing vigor to cause as many as possible to apostatize.

"Shaking" or "sifting" is a figurative expression that designates a particular experience of selection and apostasy in the people of God. As a part of threshing, grain is shaken in a sieve so that broken kernels, husks, and foreign particles fall through the mesh, and the chaff is blown away.

Likewise, in the final stage of the history of the church, a shaking will occur among the members of the church. The basic causes for the falling away will be the following: 1. religious care-

65

lessness and indifference; 2. persecution because of the enforcement of Sunday laws; 3. failure on the part of some to accept the message of Christ to the Laodicean church, a message of repentance and reform; 4. voluntary superficiality of knowledge in respect to divine truth, so that false doctrines deceive.

One tragic result of the shaking, which is even now in progress and will continue and increase, will be the apostasy of some even in outstanding positions. Certain of these will become the worst enemies of the truth and of the people of God. But no one who maintains a life of complete consecration and of true communion with God needs to be afraid of this process.

DESCRIPTION OF THE PROCESS

"God is now sifting His people, testing their purposes and their motives. Many will be but as chaff—no wheat, no value in them."— 4T 51.

"Satan has come down with great power to work with all deceivableness of unrighteousness in them that perish; and everything that can be shaken will be shaken, and those things that cannot be shaken will remain."—9T 62 (3TT 312).

"God is sifting His people. He will have a clean and holy church. We cannot read the heart of man. But the Lord has provided means to keep the church pure."—1T 99.

"An angel flying in the midst of heaven put the standard of Immanuel into many hands, while a mighty general cried out with a loud voice: 'Come into line. Let those who are loyal to the commandments of God and the testimony of Christ now take their position. Come out from among them, and be ye separate, and touch not the unclean, and I will receive you, and will be a Father unto you, and ye shall be My sons and daughters. Let all who will come up to the help of the Lord, to the help of the Lord against the mighty.' "—8T 41 (3TT 224).

CAUSES

1. Carelessness and indifference

"Thou art lukewarm." Revelation 3:16.

"My attention was then turned to the company I had seen, who were mightily shaken. I was shown those whom I had before seen weeping and praying in agony of spirit. The company of guardian angels around them had been doubled, and they were clothed with an armor from their head to their feet. They moved in exact order, like a company of soldiers. Their countenances expressed the severe conflict which they had endured, the agonizing struggle they had passed through. Yet their features, marked with severe internal anguish, now shone with the light and glory of heaven. They had obtained the victory, and it called forth from them the deepest gratitude and holy, sacred joy.

"The numbers of this company had lessened. Some had been shaken out and left by the way. The careless and indifferent, who did not join with those who prized victory and salvation enough to perseveringly plead and agonize for it, did not obtain it, and they were left behind in darkness, and their places were immediately filled by others taking hold of the truth and coming into the ranks. Evil angels still pressed around them, but could have no power over them. . . .

"I asked what had made this great change. An angel answered, 'It is the latter rain, the refreshing from the presence of the Lord, the loud cry of the third angel.' "—EW 271.

2. Persecution because of the enforcement of the Sunday law

"The words of Paul will be literally fulfilled: 'All that will live godly in Christ Jesus shall suffer persecution.' 2 Timothy 3:12. As the defenders of truth refuse to honor the Sunday-sabbath, some of them will be thrust into prison, some will be exiled, some will be treated as slaves. . . .

"As the storm approaches, a large class who have professed faith in the third angel's message, but have not been sanctified through obedience to the truth, abandon their position and join the ranks of the opposition."—GC 608.

"The mighty shaking has commenced and will go on, and all will be shaken out who are not willing to take a bold and unyielding stand for the truth and to sacrifice for God and His cause."—EW 50.

"The members of the church will individually be tested and proved. They will be placed in circumstances where they will be forced to bear witness for the truth. Many will be called to speak before councils and in courts of justice, perhaps separately and alone. The experience which would have helped them in this emergency they have neglected to obtain, and their souls are burdened with remorse for wasted opportunities and neglected privileges."—5T 463 (2TT 164).

"Soon God's people will be tested by fiery trials, and the great proportion of those who now appear to be genuine and true will prove to be base metal. Instead of being strengthened and confirmed by opposition, threats, and abuse, they will cowardly take the side of the opposers."—5T 136 (2TT 31).

3. Rejection of the Laodicean message

"Because thou art lukewarm," says Jesus, the Faithful Witness, "and neither cold nor hot, I will spew thee out of My mouth." Revelation 3:16. Those who remain indifferent and do not heed this admonition of Christ will be separated from the church during the shaking.

"I asked the meaning of the shaking I had seen and was shown that it would be caused by the straight testimony called forth by the counsel of the True Witness to the Laodiceans. This will have its effect upon the heart of the receiver, and will lead him to exalt the standard and pour forth the straight truth. Some will not bear this straight testimony. They will rise up against it, and this is what will cause a shaking among God's people.

"I saw that the testimony of the True Witness has not been half heeded. The solemn testimony upon which the destiny of the church hangs has been lightly esteemed, if not entirely disregarded. This testimony must work deep repentance; all who truly receive it will obey it and be purified."—EW 270.

4. Superficial knowledge that causes many to be deceived by false doctrines

" 'I will have upon the ground, [says Satan,] as my agents, men holding false doctrines mingled with just enough truth to deceive souls. I will also have unbelieving ones present who will express doubts in regard to the Lord's messages of warning to His church. Should the people read and believe these admonitions, we could have little hope of overcoming them. But if we can divert their attention from these warnings, they will remain ignorant of our power and cunning, and we shall secure them in our ranks at last.' "—TM 475.

"The days are fast approaching when there will be great perplexity and confusion. Satan, clothed in angel robes, will deceive, if possible, the very elect. There will be gods many and lords many. Every wind of doctrine will be blowing. . . . The Lord has faithful servants, who in the shaking, testing time will be disclosed to view."—5T 80, 81.

"God's Spirit has illuminated every page of Holy Writ, but there are those upon whom it makes little impression, because it is imperfectly understood. When the shaking comes, by the introduction of false theories, these surface readers, anchored nowhere, are like shifting sand."—TM 112.

"Those who continue to hold these spiritualistic theories [pantheistic views] will surely spoil their Christian experience, sever their connection with God, and lose eternal life.

"The sophistries regarding God and nature that are flooding the world with skepticism are the inspiration of the fallen foe, who is himself a Bible student, who knows the truth that it is essential for the people to receive, and whose study it is to divert minds from the great truths given to prepare them for what is coming upon the world."—8T 292 (3TT 270).

"The experience of the past will be repeated. In the future, Satan's superstitions will assume new forms. Errors will be presented in a pleasing and flattering manner. False theories, clothed with garments of light, will be presented to God's people. Thus Satan will try to deceive, if possible, the very elect. Most seducing influences will be exerted; minds will be hypnotized."—8T 293 (3TT 271).

"When the law of God is made void the church will be sifted by fiery trials, and a larger proportion than we now anticipate, will give heed to seducing spirits and doctrines of devils. Instead of being strengthened when brought into strait places, many prove that they are not living branches of the True Vine; they bore no fruit, and the husbandman taketh them away."—2SM 368.

THE TIME

"I saw that we are now in the shaking time."—1T 429.

"The mighty shaking has commenced and will go on, and all will be shaken out who are not willing to take a bold and unyielding stand for the truth and to sacrifice for God and His cause."—EW 50.

"I saw that we are now in the shaking time. Satan is working with all his power to wrest souls from the hand of Christ and cause them to trample underfoot the Son of God. An angel slowly and emphatically repeated these words: 'Of how much sorer punishment, suppose ye, shall he be thought worthy, who hath trodden underfoot the Son of God, and hath counted the blood of the covenant, wherewith he was sanctified, an unholy thing, and hath done despite unto the Spirit of grace?' Character is being developed. Angels of God are weighing moral worth. God is testing and proving His people. These words were presented to me by the angel: 'Take heed, brethren, lest there be in any of you an evil heart of unbelief, in departing from the living God. But exhort one another daily, while it is called today; lest any of you be hardened through the deceitfulness of sin. For we are made partakers of Christ, if we hold the beginning of our confidence steadfast unto the end.' "—1T 429.

"God is now sifting His people, testing their purposes and their motives. Many will be but as chaff—no wheat, no value in them." —4T 51.

DIRECTIONS ON HOW TO AVOID FALLING

The apostle Paul admonishes: "Let him that thinketh he standeth take heed lest he fall." 1 Corinthians 10:12. All of us will be tried, but none of us needs to fall.

We may pass triumphantly through the test of the shaking if we will maintain unbroken our contact with heaven. This all may do by Bible study and prayer, constantly yielding to God's will as revealed in the Scriptures and the spirit of prophecy, and by denial of self in service for God and others.

With our spiritual lifeline thus intact, nothing and nobody can separate us from the love of God or from the supreme Source of our strength, the Lord Jesus. The apostle asked: "Who shall separate us from the love of Christ? shall tribulation, or distress, or persecution, or famine, or nakedness, or peril, or sword?" He enumerates here the worst calamities of life. And then he answers with emphasis and complete surety: "Nay, in all these things we are more than conquerors through Him that loved us. For I am persuaded, that neither death, nor life, nor angels, nor principalities, nor powers, nor things present, nor things to come, nor height, nor depth, nor any other creature, shall be able to separate us from the love of God, which is in Christ Jesus our Lord." Romans 8:35-39.

Thank God for this blessed certainty! The inspired pen fills in further details of the struggle with the same assurances to those who will persevere:

"I saw some, with strong faith and agonizing cries, pleading with God. Their countenances were pale and marked with deep anxiety, expressive of their internal struggle. Firmness and great earnestness was expressed in their countenances; large drops of perspiration fell from their foreheads. Now and then their faces would light up with the marks of God's approbation, and again the same solemn, earnest, anxious look would settle upon them.

"Evil angels crowded around, pressing darkness upon them to shut out Jesus from their view, that their eyes might be drawn to the darkness that surrounded them, and thus they be led to distrust God and murmur against Him. Their only safety was in keeping their eyes directed upward."—EW 269.

"We are in the shaking time, the time when everything that can be shaken will be shaken. The Lord will not excuse those who know the truth if they do not in word and deed obey His commands. If we make no effort to win souls to Christ we shall be held responsible for the work we might have done, but did not do because of our spiritual indolence. Those who belong to the Lord's kingdom must work earnestly for the saving of souls. They must do their part to bind up the law and seal it among the disciples."—6T 332 (2TT 547, 548).

Regarding the overcomers we are told:

"They moved in exact order, like a company of soldiers. Their countenances expressed the severe conflict which they had endured, the agonizing struggle they had passed through. Yet their features, marked with severe internal anguish, now shone with the light and glory of heaven. They had obtained the victory, and it called forth from them the deepest gratitude and holy, sacred joy."—EW 271.

"In the mighty sifting soon to take place we shall be better able to measure the strength of Israel. The signs reveal that the time is near when the Lord will manifest that His fan is in His hand, and He will thoroughly purge His floor.

"The days are fast approaching when there will be great perplexity and confusion. Satan, clothed in angel robes, will deceive, if possible, the very elect. There will be gods many and lords many. Every wind of doctrine will be blowing. Those who have rendered supreme homage to 'science falsely so called' will not be the leaders then. Those who have trusted to intellect, genius, or talent will not then stand at the head of rank and file. They did not keep pace with the light. Those who have proved themselves unfaithful will not then be entrusted with the flock. In the last solemn work few great men will be engaged. They are self-sufficient, independent of God, and He cannot use them. The Lord has faithful servants, who in the shaking, testing time will be disclosed to view. There are precious ones now hidden who have not bowed the knee to Baal. They have not had the light which has been shining in a concentrated blaze upon you. But it may be under a rough and uninviting exterior the pure brightness of a genuine Christian character will be revealed. In the daytime we look toward heaven but do not see the stars. They are there, fixed in the firmament, but the eye cannot distinguish them. In the night we behold their genuine luster.

"The time is not far distant when the test will come to every soul. The mark of the beast will be urged upon us. Those who have step by step yielded to worldly demands and conformed to worldly customs will not find it a hard matter to yield to the powers that be, rather than subject themselves to derision, insult, threatened imprisonment, and death. The contest is between the commandments of God and the commandments of men. In this time the gold will be separated from the dross in the church. True godliness will be clearly distinguished from the appearance and tinsel of it. Many a star that we have admired for its brilliancy will then go out in darkness. Chaff like a cloud will be borne away on the wind, even from places where we see only floors of rich wheat. All who assume the ornaments of the sanctuary, but are not clothed with Christ's righteousness, will appear in the shame of their own nakedness."—5T 80, 81.

"Those who have had great light and precious privileges, but have not improved them, will, under one pretext or another, go out from us. *Not having received the love of the truth, they will be taken in the delusions of the enemy;* they will give heed to seducing spirits and doctrines of devils, and will depart from the faith. But, on the other hand, when the storm of persecution really breaks upon us, the true sheep will hear the true Shepherd's voice. Self-denying efforts will be put forth to save the lost, and many who have strayed from the fold will come back to follow the great Shepherd. The people of God will draw together and present to the enemy a united front. In view of the common peril, *strife for supremacy will cease;* there will be no disputing as to who shall be accounted greatest. No one of the true believers will say: 'I am of Paul; and I of Apollos; and I of Cephas.' *The testimony of one and all will be: 'I cleave unto Christ;* I rejoice in Him as my personal Saviour."—6T 400, 401.

CHURCH WILL NOT FALL; SINNERS WILL BE SIFTED OUT

"Satan will work his miracles to deceive; he will set up his power as supreme. The church may appear as about to fall, but it does not fall. It remains, while the sinners in Zion will be sifted out—the chaff separated from the precious wheat. This is a terrible ordeal, but nevertheless it must take place. None but those who have been overcoming by the blood of the Lamb and the word of their testimony will be found with the loyal and true, without spot or stain of sin, without guile in their mouths. We must be divested of our self-righteousness and arrayed in the righteousness of Christ."— 2SM 380.

CHAPTER 5

THE FINISHING OF GOD'S WORK
—THE LOUD CRY

Synthesis—Description—A special time for a more clear and
direct message—A rapid and miraculous work—Benefits of
the controversy—Satan's opposition to the loud cry—False
religious revivals—Two conditions necessary for finishing
the work.

SYNTHESIS

SIMULTANEOUSLY with revival and reformation within
the church, the sealing and shaking, and the reception of the latter rain, the people of God will undertake their evangelistic work
with special force and fervor.

The seer of Patmos beheld all this in the form of three angels
sweeping across heaven to proclaim in a loud voice three messages. Revelation 14:6-10.

"Here is shown the nature of the work of the people of God.
They have a message of so great importance that they are represented
as flying in the presentation of it to the world. They are holding in
their hands the bread of life for a famishing world. The love of
Christ constraineth them. *This is the last message. There are no*
more to follow, no more invitations of mercy to be given after this
message shall have done its work."—5T 206, 207.

In chapter 18, verse 1, another angel is described, who comes
down from heaven with great power, and the earth is lightened
with his glory. This angel does not represent a new message, but
a new power. This will swell the preaching of the three messages
into the loud cry, making them audible even to the utmost parts

of the earth. And in an extraordinarily brief time the work will be finished. The message of the fall of Babylon and the call for the faithful to come out of her will be given in a clear and direct manner, without evasions.

This will stir up persecution and controversy, but the Lord will make bare His holy arm to accomplish a marvelous work. In doing this He will use every worker and believer emptied of self and filled with the Spirit. The church will throw off its apathy, and all will participate in the task of saving souls. Wrote the messenger of the Lord:

"It is not alone by men in high positions of responsibility, not alone by men holding positions on boards or committees, not alone by the managers of our sanitariums and publishing houses, that the work is to be done which will cause the earth to be filled with the knowledge of the Lord as the waters cover the sea. *This work can be accomplished only by the whole church acting their part under the guidance and in the power of God.*"—8T 47.

DESCRIPTION

The Bible gives us unqualified promises regarding the completion of the gospel commission: "For He will finish the work, and cut it short in righteousness: because a short work will the Lord make upon the earth." Romans 9:28. "And this gospel of the kingdom shall be preached in all the world for a witness unto all nations; and then shall the end come." Matthew 24:14. "In the days of the voice of the seventh angel, when he shall begin to sound, the mystery of God should be finished." Revelation 10:7.

"Then will the message of the third angel swell to a loud cry, and the whole earth will be lightened with the glory of the Lord."—6T 401.

"The message loses none of its force in the angel's onward flight, for John sees it increasing in strength and power until the whole earth is lightened with its glory. The course of God's commandment-keeping people is onward, ever onward. The message of truth that we bear must go to nations, tongues, and peoples. Soon it will go with a loud voice, and the earth will be lightened with its glory. Are we preparing for this great outpouring of the Spirit of God?"—5T 383.

"Then I saw another mighty angel commissioned to descend to

the earth, to unite his voice with the third angel, and give power and force to his message. Great power and glory were imparted to the angel, and as he descended, the earth was lightened with his glory. The light which attended this angel penetrated everywhere, as he cried mightily, with a strong voice, 'Babylon the great is fallen, is fallen, and is become the habitation of devils, and the hold of every foul spirit, and a cage of every unclean and hateful bird.' "—EW 277.

"The time of test is just upon us, for the loud cry of the third angel has already begun in the revelation of the righteousness of Christ, the sin-pardoning Redeemer. This is the beginning of the light of the angel whose glory shall fill the whole earth. For it is the work of everyone to whom the message of warning has come, to lift up Jesus, to present Him to the world as revealed in types, as shadowed in symbols, as manifested in the revelations of the prophets, as unveiled in the lessons given to His disciples and in the wonderful miracles wrought for the sons of men. Search the Scriptures; for they are they that testify of Him."—1SM 363.

"The angel who unites in the proclamation of the third angel's message is to lighten the whole earth with his glory. A work of worldwide extent and unwonted power is here foretold. The advent movement of 1840-44 was a glorious manifestation of the power of God; the first angel's message was carried to every missionary station in the world, and in some countries there was the greatest religious interest which has been witnessed in any land since the Reformation of the sixteenth century; but these are to be exceeded by the mighty movement under the last warning of the third angel."—GC 611.

A SPECIAL TIME FOR A MORE CLEAR AND DIRECT MESSAGE

A special time

" 'I saw another angel come down from heaven, having great power; and the earth was lightened with his glory. And he cried mightily with a strong voice, saying, Babylon the great is fallen, is fallen, and is become the habitation of devils, and the hold of every foul spirit, and a cage of every unclean and hateful bird.' 'And I heard another voice from heaven, saying, Come out of her, My people, that ye be not partakers of her sins, and that ye receive not of her plagues.' Revelation 18:1, 2, 4.

"This scripture points forward to a time when the announcement of the fall of Babylon, as made by the second angel of Revelation 14 (verse 8), is to be repeated, with the additional mention of the corruptions which have been entering the various organizations that constitute Babylon, since that message was first given, in the summer of 1844."—GC 603.

The work of the Reformers cited as an example

"Many reformers, in entering upon their work, determined to exercise great prudence in attacking the sins of the church and the nation. They hoped, by the example of a pure Christian life, to lead the people back to the doctrines of the Bible. But the Spirit of God came upon them as it came upon Elijah, moving him to rebuke the sins of a wicked king and an apostate people; they could not refrain from preaching the plain utterances of the Bible—doctrines which they had been reluctant to present. They were impelled to zealously declare the truth and the danger which threatened souls. The words which the Lord gave them they uttered, fearless of consequences, and the people were compelled to hear the warning.

"Thus the message of the third angel will be proclaimed. As the time comes for it to be given with greatest power, the Lord will work through humble instruments, leading the minds of those who consecrate themselves to His service. The laborers will be qualified rather by the unction of His Spirit than by the training of literary institutions. Men of faith and prayer will be constrained to go forth with holy zeal, declaring the words which God gives them. The sins of Babylon will be laid open. The fearful results of enforcing the observances of the church by civil authority, the inroads of spiritualism, the stealthy but rapid progress of the papal power—all will be unmasked. By these solemn warnings the people will be stirred. Thousands upon thousands will listen who have never heard words like these."—GC 606.

The message will arouse persecution

"The clergy will put forth almost superhuman efforts to shut away the light lest it should shine upon their flocks. By every means at their command they will endeavor to suppress the discussion of these vital questions. The church appeals to the strong arm of civil power, and, in this work, papists and Protestants unite. As the movement for Sunday enforcement becomes more bold and decided, the law will be invoked against commandment keepers. They will be threatened with fines and imprisonment, and some will be offered positions of influence, and other rewards and advantages, as inducements to renounce their faith. But their steadfast answer is: 'Show us from the Word of God our error'—the same plea that was made by Luther under similar circumstances. Those who are arraigned before the courts make a strong vindication of the truth, and some who hear them are led to take their stand to keep all the commandments of God. Thus light will be brought before thousands who otherwise would know nothing of these truths."—GC 607.

"The words of Paul will be literally fulfilled: 'All that will live godly in Christ Jesus shall suffer persecution.' 2 Timothy 3:12. As the defenders of truth refuse to honor the Sunday-sabbath, some of them will be thrust into prison, some will be exiled, some will be treated as slaves. To human wisdom all this now seems impossible; but as the restraining Spirit of God shall be withdrawn from men, and they shall be under the control of Satan, who hates the divine precepts, there will be strange developments. The heart can be very cruel when God's fear and love are removed."—GC 608.

Temporary consternation and dismay

"In this time of persecution the faith of the Lord's servants will be tried. They have faithfully given the warning, looking to God and to His Word alone. God's Spirit, moving upon their hearts, has constrained them to speak. Stimulated with holy zeal, and with the divine impulse strong upon them, they entered upon the performance of their duties without coldly calculating the consequences of speaking to the people the word which the Lord had given them. They have not consulted their temporal interests, nor sought to preserve their reputation or their lives. Yet when the storm of opposition and reproach bursts upon them, some, overwhelmed with consternation, will be ready to exclaim: 'Had we foreseen the consequences of our words, we would have held our peace.' They are hedged in with difficulties. Satan assails them with fierce temptations. The work which they have undertaken seems far beyond their ability to accomplish. They are threatened with destruction. The enthusiasm which animated them is gone; yet they cannot turn back. Then, feeling their utter helplessness, they flee to the Mighty One for strength. They remember that the words which they have spoken were not theirs, but His who bade them give the warning. God put the truth into their hearts, and they could not forbear to proclaim it.

"The same trials have been experienced by men of God in ages past. Wycliffe, Huss, Luther, Tyndale, Baxter, Wesley, urged that all doctrines be brought to the test of the Bible and declared that they would renounce everything which it condemned. Against these men persecution raged with relentless fury; yet they ceased not to declare the truth."—GC 608, 609.

The message will be proclaimed with faith and power

"The Lord gives a special truth for the people in an emergency. Who dare refuse to publish it? He commands His servants to present the last invitation of mercy to the world. They cannot remain silent, except at the peril of their souls. Christ's ambassadors have nothing to do with consequences. . . .

"As the opposition rises to a fiercer height, the servants of God are again perplexed; for it seems to them that they have brought the crisis. But conscience and the Word of God assure them that their course is right; and although the trials continue, they are strengthened to bear them. The contest grows closer and sharper, but their faith and courage rise with the emergency. Their testimony is: 'We dare not tamper with God's Word, dividing His holy law; calling one portion essential and another nonessential, to gain the favor of the world. The Lord whom we serve is able to deliver us. Christ has conquered the powers of earth; and shall we be afraid of a world already conquered?' "—GC 609, 610.

"The time is fast approaching when those who choose to obey God rather than man will be made to feel the hand of oppression. Shall we then dishonor God by keeping silent while His holy commandments are trodden underfoot?"—5T 716 (2TT 323).

"When the storm of persecution really breaks upon us, the true sheep will hear the true Shepherd's voice. Self-denying efforts will be put forth to save the lost, and many who have strayed from the fold will come back to follow the great Shepherd. The people of God will draw together and present to the enemy a united front. In view of the common peril, strife for supremacy will cease. . . .

"Thus will the truth be brought into practical life, and thus will be answered the prayer of Christ, uttered just before His humiliation and death: 'That they all may be one; as Thou, Father, art in Me, and I in Thee, that they also may be one in Us: that the world may believe that Thou hast sent Me.' John 17:21. The love of Christ, the love of our brethren, will testify to the world that we have been with Jesus and learned of Him. Then will the message of the third angel swell to a loud cry, and the whole earth will be lightened with the glory of the Lord."—6T 401.

A RAPID AND MIRACULOUS WORK

"The great work of the gospel is not to close with less manifestation of the power of God than marked its opening. The prophecies which were fulfilled in the outpouring of the former rain at the opening of the gospel are again to be fulfilled in the latter rain at its close. Here are 'the times of refreshing' to which the apostle Peter looked forward when he said: 'Repent ye therefore, and be converted, that your sins may be blotted out, when the times of refreshing shall come from the presence of the Lord; and He shall send Jesus.' Acts 3:19, 20.

"Servants of God, with their faces lighted up and shining with holy consecration, will hasten from place to place to proclaim the message from heaven. By thousands of voices, all over the earth, the warning will be given. Miracles will be wrought, the sick will be healed, and signs and wonders will follow the believers. Satan also works with lying wonders, even bringing down fire from heaven in the sight of men. Revelation 13:13. Thus the inhabitants of the earth will be brought to take their stand.

"The message will be carried not so much by argument as by the deep conviction of the Spirit of God. The arguments have been presented. The seed has been sown, and now it will spring up and bear fruit. The publications distributed by missionary workers have exerted their influence, yet many whose minds were impressed have been prevented from fully comprehending the truth or from yielding obedience. Now the rays of light penetrate everywhere, the truth is seen in its clearness, and the honest children of God sever the bands which have held them. Family connections, church relations, are powerless to stay them now. Truth is more precious than all besides. Notwithstanding the agencies combined against the truth, a large number take their stand upon the Lord's side."—GC 611, 612.

"When the final warning shall be given, it will arrest the attention of these leading men through whom the Lord is now working, and some of them will accept it, and will stand with the people of God through the time of trouble."—GC 611.

"The work will be similar to that of the Day of Pentecost. As the 'former rain' was given, in the outpouring of the Holy Spirit at the opening of the gospel, to cause the upspringing of the precious seed, so the 'latter rain' will be given at its close for the ripening of the harvest."—GC 611.

"A compelling power moved the honest, while the manifestation of the power of God brought a fear and restraint upon their unbelieving relatives and friends so that they dared not, neither had they the power to, hinder those who felt the work of the Spirit of God upon them."—EW 278.

"God will use ways and means by which it will be seen that He is taking the reins in His own hands. The workers will be surprised by the simple means that He will use to bring about and perfect His work of righteousness."—TM 300.

"Through most wonderful workings of divine providence, mountains of difficulty will be removed and cast into the sea. The message that means so much to the dwellers upon the earth will be heard and understood. Men will know what is truth. Onward and still onward the work will advance until the whole earth shall have been warned, and then shall the end come."—9T 96 (3TT 332).

"The light that was shed upon the waiting ones penetrated everywhere, and those in the churches who had any light, who had not heard and rejected the three messages, obeyed the call and left the fallen churches."—EW 278.

"The last call was carried even to the poor slaves, and the pious among them poured forth their songs of rapturous joy at the prospect of their happy deliverance. Their masters could not check them; fear and astonishment kept them silent. Mighty miracles were wrought, the sick were healed, and signs and wonders followed the believers."—EW 278.

"The light of truth will shine forth in clear, strong rays, and, as in the time of the apostles, many souls will turn from error to truth. The earth will be lighted with the glory of the Lord."—9T 46 (3TT 308).

"Notwithstanding the agencies combined against the truth, a large number take their stand upon the Lord's side."—GC 612.

"He will call men from the plow and from other occupations to give the last note of warning to perishing souls. There are many ways in which to work for the Master, and the Great Teacher will open the understanding of these workers, enabling them to see wondrous things in His Word."—9T 170 (3TT 369).

"I saw that God has His agents, even among the rulers. And some of them will yet be converted to the truth. They are now acting the part that God would have them. When Satan works through his agents, propositions are made, that, if carried out, would impede the work of God and produce great evil. The good angels move upon these agents of God to oppose such propositions with strong reasons, which Satan's agents cannot resist. A few of God's agents will have power to bear down a great mass of evil. Thus the work will go on until the third message has done its work, and at the loud cry of the third angel, these agents will have an opportunity to receive the truth, and some of them will be converted, and endure with the saints through the time of trouble."—1T 203 (1TT 74).

BENEFITS OF THE CONTROVERSY

"God means that testing truth shall be brought to the front and become a subject of examination and discussion, even if it is through the contempt placed upon it. The minds of the people must be agitated. Every controversy, every reproach, every slander, will be God's means of provoking inquiry and awakening minds that otherwise would slumber."—5T 453 (2TT 153).

"But as the question of enforcing Sunday observance is widely agitated, the event so long doubted and disbelieved is seen to be approaching, and the third message will produce an effect which it could not have had before."—GC 605, 606.

"The efforts made to retard the progress of truth will serve to extend it. The excellence of truth is more clearly seen from every successive point from which it may be viewed. Error requires disguise and concealment. It clothes itself in angel robes, and every manifestation of its real character lessens its chance of success."—5T 454 (2TT 154).

SATAN'S OPPOSITION TO THE LOUD CRY

"The people of God are directed to the Scriptures as their safeguard against the influence of false teachers and the delusive power of spirits of darkness. Satan employs every possible device to prevent men from obtaining a knowledge of the Bible; for its plain utterances reveal his deceptions. At every revival of God's work the prince of evil is aroused to more intense activity; he is now putting forth his utmost efforts for a final struggle against Christ and His followers. The last great delusion is soon to open before us."—GC 593.

"So it will be in the great final conflict of the controversy between righteousness and sin. While new life and light and power are descending from on high upon the disciples of Christ, a new life is springing up from beneath, and energizing the agencies of Satan. Intensity is taking possession of every earthly element. With a subtlety gained through centuries of conflict, the prince of evil works under a disguise. He appears clothed as an angel of light, and multitudes are 'giving heed to seducing spirits, and doctrines of devils.'"—DA 257.

"The powers of Satan are at work to keep minds diverted from eternal realities. The enemy has arranged matters to suit his own purposes. Worldly business, sports, the fashions of the day—these things occupy the minds of men and women."—9T 43 (3TT 306).

"Satan delights in war, for it excites the worst passions of the soul and then sweeps into eternity its victims steeped in vice and blood. It is his object to incite the nations to war against one another, for he can thus divert the minds of the people from the work of preparation to stand in the day of God."—GC 589.

FALSE RELIGIOUS REVIVALS

"Notwithstanding the widespread declension of faith and piety, there are true followers of Christ in these churches [the popular churches of today]. Before the final visitation of God's judgments upon the earth there will be among the people of the Lord such a revival of primitive godliness as has not been witnessed since apostolic times. The Spirit and power of God will be poured out upon His children. At that time many will separate themselves from those churches in which the love of this world has supplanted love for God and His Word. Many, both of ministers and people, will gladly accept those great truths which God has caused to be proclaimed at this time to prepare a people for the Lord's second coming. The enemy of souls desires to hinder this work; and before the time for such a movement shall come, he will endeavor to prevent it by introducing a counterfeit. In those churches which he can bring under his deceptive power he will make it appear that God's special blessing is poured out; there will be manifest what is thought to be great religious interest. Multitudes will exult that God is working marvelously for them, when the work is that of another spirit. Under a religious guise, Satan will seek to extend his influence over the Christian world.

"In many of the revivals which have occurred during the last half century, the same influences have been at work, to a greater or less degree, that will be manifest in the more extensive movements of the future."—GC 464.

"While God's agents of mercy work through consecrated human beings, Satan sets his agencies in operation, laying under tribute all who will submit to his control."—9T 47 (3TT 308).

"And as the spirits will profess faith in the Bible, and manifest respect for the institutions of the church, their work will be accepted as a manifestation of divine power."—GC 588.

"Now the Spirit speaketh expressly, that in the latter times some shall depart from the faith, giving heed to seducing spirits, and doctrines of devils." 1 Timothy 4:1.

TWO CONDITIONS NECESSARY FOR
FINISHING THE WORK

The Lord has definitely promised that the proclamation of the third angel's message will soon swell into the loud cry. The glorious finishing of the work of evangelizing the whole world is assured by a series of divine promises that are at the same time prophecies. The angel of Revelation 18, represented as coming down with great power, lightens the whole earth with the glory of God; and in a short time every nation, kindred, tongue, and people may know the truth and make their decision.

The consummation of the work of the gospel is primarily a divine work. God has promised it, and He has ample resources to accomplish it.

But in order to carry out His marvelous design, the Lord uses human beings as instruments. The three angels of Revelation 14 represent God's people on the march, engaged in the fulfillment of their gospel commission.

All that is necessary in order for the Most High to make bare His holy arm is that the people whom He desires to use comply with two indispensable conditions: *sanctification* and *activity*.

On the eve of Israel's great test of reliance on God's power—the crossing of the Jordan—Joshua gave the people, by divine command, this significant order: "Sanctify yourselves: for tomorrow the Lord will do wonders among you." Joshua 3:5. The work can never be done by human effort. It must be wrought by a miracle, as a result of the outpouring of the Holy Spirit. "Not by might, nor by power, but by My Spirit, saith the Lord of hosts." Zechariah 4:6.

But as we have already seen, the Spirit is poured out only when the heart is ready to receive Him, when sanctification is complete, when sin has been confessed and forsaken, when self is dead, when the spirit of supremacy is banished, when meekness, humility, and full consecration characterize believers.

Now the second condition, activity—dedicated and enthusiastic activity. The Lord has commanded: "Go ye into all the world, and preach the gospel to every creature." Mark 16:15. To each of us He says, "Go ye also into the vineyard." Matthew 20:4.

The parable of the talents explains how to use the time of our waiting for the coming of Christ—not in idle expectation but in active labor, making use of the talents He has entrusted to us. The Lord requires us to use our minds, our legs, our voices, yes, our whole being for finishing the work of harvest so that the Saviour may return.

Sanctified lives and diligent activity will convert into reality the most cheering of God's promises, affording the greatest satisfaction to those who have been faithful instruments in the Master's hands.

CHAPTER 6

PERSECUTION—
THE CONFEDERATED POWERS

Synthesis—The persecution in general—Divine protection —The rest day as the focal point—The crisis will be universal—The beast with horns like a lamb—Alliance of powers: the dragon, the beast, the false prophet, the state— The image to the beast—The mark of the beast—Sunday laws—Sunday as a day of missionary work—Only two classes—The death decree—Leaving the cities—Emergency flight from the cities—The song of victory.

SYNTHESIS

THROUGHOUT ALL AGES the deliberate plan of the enemy has been to oppose the truth, obstructing its advance by every means, including persecution. But in this time of the end Satan will multiply his efforts to the maximum. He will come down with great wrath because he knows he has but a short time. To accomplish his ends he will use governments, as well as religious and other institutions, culminating his efforts by making them impose Sunday observance by law.

The great test for the people of God will be initiated when the Sunday law is made national or federal in the United States. Soon thereafter the same law will be enforced universally.

This issue—the establishment of a religious and federal Sunday law—which occurs before the close of probation, will reach its greatest severity with a death decree, after the close of probation.

Since this subject has many aspects, we shall complete this synthesis in parts with a commentary or additional explanation under each one of the subtitles.

THE PERSECUTION IN GENERAL

The apostle Paul declares: "All that will live godly in Christ Jesus shall suffer persecution." 2 Timothy 3:12. But the righteous must not fear the persecution nor consider it a disgrace, because Christ pronounced a blessing on those who suffer and promised His special companionship and blessing in this kind of emergency. "Blessed are they which are persecuted for righteousness' sake: for theirs is the kingdom of heaven. Blessed are ye, when men shall revile you, and persecute you, and shall say all manner of evil against you falsely, for My sake. Rejoice, and be exceeding glad: for great is your reward in heaven: for so persecuted they the prophets which were before you." Matthew 5:10-12.

"No man can serve God without enlisting against himself the opposition of the hosts of darkness. Evil angels will assail him, alarmed that his influence is taking the prey from their hands. Evil men, rebuked by his example, will unite with them in seeking to separate him from God by alluring temptations. When these do not succeed, then a compelling power is employed to force the conscience."—GC 610.

"There is a prospect before us of a continued struggle, at the risk of imprisonment, loss of property, and even of life itself, to defend the law of God, which is made void by the laws of men."—5T 712 (2TT 319).

"As he [Satan] influenced the heathen nations to destroy Israel, so in the near future he will stir up the wicked powers of earth to destroy the people of God. All will be required to render obedience to human edicts in violation of the divine law. Those who will be true to God and to duty will be menaced, denounced, and proscribed. They will 'be betrayed both by parents, and brethren, and kinsfolks, and friends.' "—5T 473 (2TT 176).

"The forms of religion will be continued by a people from whom the Spirit of God has been finally withdrawn; and the satanic zeal with which the prince of evil will inspire them for the accomplishment of his malignant designs, will bear the semblance of zeal for God."—GC 615.

"Satan will excite indignation against the humble minority who conscientiously refuse to accept popular customs and traditions. Men of position and reputation will join with the lawless and the vile to take counsel against the people of God. Wealth, genius, education, will combine to cover them with contempt. Persecuting rulers, ministers, and church members will conspire against them. With voice and pen, by boasts, threats, and ridicule, they will seek to overthrow their faith. By false representations and angry appeals they will stir up the passions of the people. Not having a 'Thus saith the Scriptures' to bring against the advocates of the Bible Sabbath, they will resort to oppressive enactments to supply the lack."—5T 450, 451 (2TT 150).

"And at that time [of terrible crisis] the superficial, conservative class, whose influence has steadily retarded the progress of the work, will renounce the faith and take their stand with its avowed enemies, toward whom their sympathies have long been tending."—5T 463 (2TT 164).

"As the storm approaches, a large class who have professed faith in the third angel's message, but have not been sanctified through obedience to the truth, abandon their position and join the ranks of the opposition. By uniting with the world and partaking of its spirit, they have come to view matters in nearly the same light; and when the test is brought, they are prepared to choose the easy, popular side. Men of talent and pleasing address, who once rejoiced in the truth, employ their powers to deceive and mislead souls. They become the most bitter enemies of their former brethren. When Sabbath keepers are brought before the courts to answer for their faith, these apostates are the most efficient agents of Satan to misrepresent and accuse them, and by false reports and insinuations to stir up the rulers against them."—GC 608.

"These apostates will then manifest the most bitter enmity, doing all in their power to oppress and malign their former brethren and to excite indignation against them. This day is just before us."—5T 463 (2TT 164).

"In amazement they [the people in general] hear the testimony that Babylon is the church, fallen because of her errors and sins, because of her rejection of the truth sent to her from heaven. As the people go to their former teachers with the eager inquiry, Are these things so? the ministers present fables, prophesy smooth things, to soothe their fears and quiet the awakened conscience. But since many refuse to be satisfied with the mere authority of men and demand a plain 'Thus saith the Lord,' the popular ministry, like the Pharisees of old, filled with anger as their authority is questioned, will denounce the message as of Satan and stir up the sin-loving multitudes to revile and persecute those who proclaim it."—GC 606, 607.

"And the dragon was wroth with the woman, and went to

make war with the remnant of her seed, which keep the commandments of God, and have the testimony of Jesus Christ." Revelation 12:17.

"This small remnant, unable to defend themselves in the deadly conflict with the powers of earth that are marshaled by the dragon host, make God their defense."—5T 213 (2TT 67).

"The eye of God, looking down the ages, was fixed upon the crisis which His people are to meet, when earthly powers shall be arrayed against them."—GC 634.

"The Lord showed me that a great work must be done for His people before they could stand in the battle in the day of the Lord." —EW 69.

"The time is not far distant when the test will come to every soul. The mark of the beast will be urged upon us. Those who have step by step yielded to worldly demands and conformed to worldly customs will not find it a hard matter to yield to the powers that be, rather than subject themselves to derision, insult, threatened imprisonment, and death. The contest is between the commandments of God and the commandments of men. In this time the gold will be separated from the dross in the church. True godliness will be clearly distinguished from the appearance and tinsel of it. Many a star that we have admired for its brilliancy will then go out in darkness."— 5T 81.

"The members of the church will individually be tested and proved. They will be placed in circumstances where they will be forced to bear witness for the truth. Many will be called to speak before councils and in courts of justice, perhaps separately and alone."—5T 463 (2TT 164).

"The National Reform movement,* exercising the power of religious legislation, will, when fully developed, manifest the same intolerance and oppression that have prevailed in past ages. Human councils then assumed the prerogatives of Deity, crushing under their despotic power liberty of conscience; and imprisonment, exile, and death followed for those who opposed their dictates. If popery or its principles shall again be legislated into power, the fires of persecution will be rekindled against those who will not sacrifice conscience and the truth in deference to popular errors. This evil is on the point of realization."—5T 712 (2TT 319).

*An agency of the churches in 1889 promoting Sunday legislation in the United State of America.

"While Satan seeks to destroy those who honor God's law, he will cause them to be accused as lawbreakers, as men who are dishonoring God and bringing judgments upon the world."—GC 591.

DIVINE PROTECTION

God has promised His special protection throughout the storm. Even so it is possible that before the close of probation some will suffer martyrdom. But once probation has closed and the time of great trouble begins it appears that none of God's children will lose their lives. They will be miraculously guarded and cared for by the Lord and His angels.

"Because thou hast kept the word of My patience, I also will keep thee from the hour of temptation, which shall come upon all the world, to try them that dwell upon the earth." Revelation 3:10.

"Fearful tests and trials await the people of God. The spirit of war is stirring the nations from one end of the earth to the other. But in the midst of the time of trouble that is coming,—a time of trouble such as has not been since there was a nation,—God's chosen people will stand unmoved. Satan and his host cannot destroy them, for angels that excel in strength will protect them."—9T 17 (3TT 285).

"Though enemies may thrust them [God's faithful] into prison, yet dungeon walls cannot cut off the communication between their souls and Christ. One who sees their every weakness, who is acquainted with every trial, is above all earthly powers; and angels will come to them in lonely cells, bringing light and peace from heaven. The prison will be as a palace; for the rich in faith dwell there, and the gloomy walls will be lighted up with heavenly light as when Paul and Silas prayed and sang praises at midnight in the Philippian dungeon."—GC 627.

"Will the Lord forget His people in this trying hour? Did He forget faithful Noah when judgments were visited upon the antediluvian world? Did He forget Lot when the fire came down from heaven to consume the cities of the plain? Did He forget Joseph surrounded by idolaters in Egypt? Did He forget Elijah when the oath of Jezebel threatened him with the fate of the prophets of Baal? Did He forget Jeremiah in the dark and dismal pit of his prison house? Did He forget the three worthies in the fiery furnace? or Daniel in the den of lions?"—GC 626.

"God would not suffer the wicked to destroy those who are

expecting translation and who would not bow to the decree of the beast or receive his mark. I saw that if the wicked were permitted to slay the saints, Satan and all his evil host, and all who hate God, would be gratified. And oh, what a triumph it would be for his satanic majesty to have power, in the last closing struggle, over those who had so long waited to behold Him whom they loved! Those who have mocked at the idea of the saints' going up will witness the care of God for His people and behold their glorious deliverance." —EW 284.

THE REST DAY AS THE FOCAL POINT

Since the observance of Sabbath is the external manifestation of the seal of God, and the observance of Sunday under law becomes the mark of the beast, and because the first acknowledges loyalty to the Creator and the second to Rome and the satanic power, it naturally follows that the day of rest becomes the great central theme of the controversy in the last days.

"And the dragon [the devil and his agents]," says the prophet John, "was wroth with the woman [God's church], and went to make war with the remnant of her seed, which keep the commandments of God, and have the testimony of Jesus Christ." Revelation 12:17.

"The remnant church will be brought into great trial and distress. Those who keep the commandments of God and the faith of Jesus will feel the ire of the dragon and his hosts."—5T 472 (2TT 175, 176).

"As the Sabbath has become the special point of controversy throughout Christendom, and religious and secular authorities have combined to enforce the observance of the Sunday, the persistent refusal of a small minority to yield to the popular demand will make them objects of universal execration. It will be urged that the few who stand in opposition to an institution of the church and a law of the state ought not to be tolerated; that it is better for them to suffer than for whole nations to be thrown into confusion and lawlessness."—GC 615.

"Those who honor the Bible Sabbath will be denounced as enemies of law and order, as breaking down the moral restraints of society, causing anarchy and corruption, and calling down the judgments of God upon the earth. Their conscientious scruples will be pronounced obstinacy, stubbornness, and contempt of authority. They will be accused of disaffection toward the government. Ministers who deny the obligation of the divine law will present from the pulpit the duty of yielding obedience to the civil authorities as ordained of God. In legislative halls and courts of justice, commandment keepers will be misrepresented and condemned. A false coloring will be given to their words; the worst construction will be put upon their motives."—GC 592.

"The dignitaries of church and state will unite to bribe, persuade, or compel all classes to honor the Sunday. The lack of divine authority will be supplied by oppressive enactments."—GC 592.

"And then the great deceiver will persuade men that those who serve God are causing these evils. The class that have provoked the displeasure of Heaven will charge all their troubles upon those whose obedience to God's commandments is a perpetual reproof to transgressors. It will be declared that men are offending God by the violation of the Sunday sabbath; that this sin has brought calamities which will not cease until Sunday observance shall be strictly enforced; and that those who present the claims of the fourth commandment, thus destroying reverence for Sunday, are troublers of the people, preventing their restoration to divine favor and temporal prosperity. . . . As the wrath of the people shall be excited by false charges, they will pursue a course toward God's ambassadors very similar to that which apostate Israel pursued toward Elijah."—GC 590.

"As the controversy extends into new fields and the minds of the people are called to God's downtrodden law, Satan is astir. The power attending the message will only madden those who oppose it. The clergy will put forth almost superhuman efforts to shut away the light lest it should shine upon their flocks. By every means at their command they will endeavor to suppress the discussion of these vital questions. The church appeals to the strong arm of civil power, and, in this work, papists and Protestants unite. As the movement for Sunday enforcement becomes more bold and decided, the law will be invoked against commandment keepers. They will be threatened with fines and imprisonment, and some will be offered positions of influence, and other rewards and advantages, as inducements to renounce their faith."—GC 607.

"And at the commencement of the [early] time of trouble, we were filled with the Holy Ghost as we went forth and proclaimed the Sabbath more fully. This enraged the churches and nominal Adventists [Adventists who have participated in the messages of the first and second angels but have rejected the third angel's message with its Sabbath emphasis], as they could not refute the Sabbath truth. And at this time God's chosen all saw clearly that we had the truth, and they came out and endured the persecution with us."— EW 33.

"Church and state are now making preparations for the future conflict. Protestants are working in disguise to bring Sunday to the front, as did the Romanists. Throughout the land the papacy is piling up her lofty and massive structures, in the secret recesses of which her former persecutions are to be repeated. And the way is preparing for the manifestation, on a grand scale, of those lying wonders by which, if it were possible, Satan would deceive even the elect."—5T 449, 450 (2TT 149).

"Men will exalt and rigidly enforce laws that are in direct opposition to the law of God. Though zealous in enforcing their own commandments, they will turn away from a plain 'Thus saith the Lord.' Exalting a spurious rest day, they will seek to force men to dishonor the law of Jehovah, the transcript of His character. Though innocent of wrongdoing, the servants of God will be given over to suffer humiliation and abuse at the hands of those who, inspired by Satan, are filled with envy and religious bigotry."—9T 229 (3TT 392, 393).

"The conflict is between the requirements of God and the requirements of the beast.. The first day, a papal institution which directly contradicts the fourth commandment, is yet to be made a test by the two-horned beast. And then the fearful warning from God declares the penalty of bowing to the beast and his image. They shall drink the wine of the wrath of God, which is poured out without mixture into the cup of His indignation."—1T 223 (1TT 79).

"Political corruption is destroying love of justice and regard for truth; and even in free America, rulers and legislators, in order to secure public favor, will yield to the popular demand for a law enforcing Sunday observance. Liberty of conscience, which has cost so great a sacrifice, will no longer be respected."—GC 592.

"The Sunday movement is now [1885] making its way in darkness. The leaders are concealing the true issue, and many who unite in the movement do not themselves see whither the undercurrent is tending. Its professions are mild and apparently Christian, but when it shall speak it will reveal the spirit of the dragon."—5T 452 (2TT 152).

"In the movements now in progress in the United States to secure for the institutions and usages of the church the support of the state, Protestants are following in the steps of papists. Nay, more, they are opening the door for the papacy to regain in Protestant

America the supremacy which she has lost in the Old World. And that which gives greater significance to this movement is the fact that the principal object contemplated is the enforcement of Sunday observance—a custom which originated with Rome, and which she claims as the sign of her authority."—GC 573.

To the Lord's messenger was given the opportunity to hear, while in vision, the actual words spoken by the great deceiver. Said Satan:

" 'But our principal concern is to silence this sect of Sabbath keepers. We must excite popular indignation against them. We will enlist great men and worldly-wise men upon our side, and induce those in authority to carry out our purposes.' "—TM 473.

"These records of the past [referring to historical cases in which Rome required various peoples to abandon the Sabbath and observe Sunday] clearly reveal the enmity of Rome toward the true Sabbath and its defenders, and the means which she employs to honor the institution of her creating. The Word of God teaches that these scenes are to be repeated as Roman Catholics and Protestants shall unite for the exaltation of the Sunday."—GC 578.

"Communications from the spirits will declare that God has sent them to convince the rejecters of Sunday of their error, affirming that the laws of the land should be obeyed as the law of God. They will lament the great wickedness in the world and second the testimony of religious teachers that the degraded state of morals is caused by the desecration of Sunday. Great will be the indignation excited against all who refuse to accept their testimony."—GC 591.

"Yet this very class [religious leaders of the world] put forth the claim that the fast-spreading corruption is largely attributable to the desecration of the so-called 'Christian sabbath,' and that the enforcement of Sunday observance would greatly improve the morals of society. This claim is especially urged in America, where the doctrine of the true Sabbath has been most widely preached."—GC 587.

"[Satan says:] 'Thus the world will become mine. I will be the ruler of the earth, the prince of the world. I will so control the minds under my power that God's Sabbath shall be a special object of contempt. A sign? *I will make the observance of the seventh day a sign of disloyalty to the authorities of earth.* Human laws will be made so stringent that men and women will not dare to observe the seventh-day Sabbath. For fear of wanting food and clothing, they will join with the world in transgressing God's law. The earth will be wholly under my dominion.' "—PK 184.

THE CRISIS WILL BE UNIVERSAL

In the symbolic portrayal of the United States of America as the second beast of Revelation 13 (with horns like a lamb), John shows that this nation will eventually reverse its benevolent policy and perform the following acts:

1. "Causeth the earth and them which dwell therein to worship the first beast [Rome]." Verse 12.

2. "Deceiveth them that dwell on the earth." Verse 14.

3. Orders "them that dwell on the earth, that they should make an image to the beast [Rome]." Verse 14.

The repeated expression "them that dwell on the earth" implies a universal work.

The United States has up to this time been the great bulwark of religious liberty. Also because of her immense wealth she has attained a position of world influence. It will be natural therefore that when this nation imposes Sunday laws and begins persecution, the rest of the nations will follow her example. In this manner the crisis will become universal.

"As America, the land of religious liberty, shall unite with the papacy in forcing the conscience and compelling men to honor the false sabbath, the people of *every country on the globe* will be led to follow her example. Our people are not half awake to do all in their power, with the facilities within their reach, to extend the message of warning."—6T 18 (2TT 373).

"In both the Old and the New World, the papacy will receive homage in the honor paid to the Sunday institution, that rests solely upon the authority of the Roman Church."—GC 579.

"This crisis will be reached when the nations shall unite in making void God's law."—5T 524.

"The substitution of the laws of men for the law of God, the exaltation, by merely human authority, of Sunday in place of the Bible Sabbath, is the last act in the drama. When this substitution becomes universal, God will reveal Himself. He will arise in His majesty to shake terribly the earth. He will come out of His place to punish the inhabitants of the world for their iniquity."—7T 141.

"The less we make direct charges against authorities and powers, the greater work we shall be able to accomplish, both in America and in foreign countries. Foreign nations will follow the example of the United States. Though she leads out, yet the same crisis will come upon our people in all parts of the world."—6T 395 (3TT 46).

"When the protection of human laws shall be withdrawn from those who honor the law of God, there will be, in different lands, a simultaneous movement for their destruction."—GC 635.

THE BEAST WITH HORNS LIKE A LAMB

In Revelation 13—key chapter in the panorama of final events —two beasts are presented. The first—with seven heads and ten horns (verses 1-10)—represents papal Rome;* the second—with two horns like a lamb (verses 11-18)—symbolizes the United States of America.

It is evident that this prophecy presents a strange paradox. Without doubt the United States has been a freedom-loving country, a veritable fortress of religious liberty. Its democratic spirit—well represented by the innocence of the lamb—its complete separation of church and state, and its high respect for individual liberties, especially the liberty of worship, has made it the mecca of all the world's oppressed. Furthermore, the Lord has seen fit to establish the world center of the Adventist Church in this privileged and powerful nation. From its generous shores men and needed resources have gone to the ends of the earth to carry the three angels' messages.

Nevertheless, this very nation in the last short hours of its history will about-face and follow in the footsteps of Rome by becoming a persecuting power. For a panoramic description of this incredible shift in policy read Revelation 13:11-18. Also turn back and read again the survey in the Introduction.

"The prophecy of Revelation 13 declares that the power represented by the beast with lamblike horns shall cause 'the earth and them which dwell therein' to worship the papacy—there symbolized by the beast 'like unto a leopard.' The beast with two horns is also to say 'to them that dwell on the earth, that they should make an image to the beast'; and, furthermore, it is to command all, 'both small and great, rich and poor, free and bond,' to receive the mark of the beast. Revelation 13:11-16. It has been shown that the United

---

*In a more precise explanation we may say that the first beast with seven heads and ten horns is a symbol of Satan working through the historical process of seven successive powers that in the course of history have opposed God and fought against His truth and His people. The prophet, using a literary figure called "synechdoche," which names the whole for the part, presents the whole beast in order to refer especially to the seventh head—at this stage, the papacy.

States is the power represented by the beast with lamblike horns, and that this prophecy will be fulfilled when the United States shall enforce Sunday observance, which Rome claims as the special acknowledgment of her supremacy."—GC 578, 579.

"One nation, and only one, meets the specifications of this prophecy; it points unmistakably to the United States of America."—GC 441.

"When the nation for which God has worked in such a marvelous manner, and over which He has spread the shield of Omnipotence, abandons Protestant principles, and through its legislature gives countenance and support to Romanism in limiting religious liberty, then God will work in His own power for His people that are true. The tyranny of Rome will be exercised, but Christ is our refuge."— TM 206.

"By the decree enforcing the institution of the papacy in violation of the law of God, our nation will disconnect herself fully from righteousness."—5T 451 (2TT 150).

"When our nation shall so abjure the principles of its government as to enact a Sunday law, Protestantism will in this act join hands with popery; it will be nothing else than giving life to the tyranny which has long been eagerly watching its opportunity to spring again into active despotism."—5T 712 (2TT 318, 319).

"When our nation, in its legislative councils, shall enact laws to bind the consciences of men in regard to their religious privileges, enforcing Sunday observance, and bringing oppressive power to bear against those who keep the seventh-day Sabbath, the law of God will, to all intents and purposes, be made void in our land; and national apostasy will be followed by national ruin."—7BC 977.

"It is at the time of the national apostasy, when, acting on the policy of Satan, the rulers of the land will rank themselves on the side of the man of sin—it is then the measure of guilt is full; the national apostasy is the signal for national ruin."—2SM 373.

"The people of the United States have been a favored people; but when they restrict religious liberty, surrender Protestantism, and give countenance to popery, the measure of their guilt will be full, and 'national apostasy' will be registered in the books of heaven. The result of this apostasy will be national ruin."—RH, May 2, 1893.

"Satan is at work through human agencies. Those who are making an effort to change the Constitution and secure a law enforcing Sunday observance little realize what will be the result. A crisis is just upon us."—5T 753 (2TT 352).

"While men are sleeping, Satan is actively arranging matters so that the Lord's people may not have mercy or justice. The Sunday movement is now making its way in darkness. The leaders are concealing the true issue, and many who unite in the movement do not themselves see whither the undercurrent is tending. Its professions are mild and apparently Christian, but when it shall speak it will reveal the spirit of the dragon."—5T 452 (2TT 152).

ALLIANCE OF POWERS: THE DRAGON, THE BEAST, THE FALSE PROPHET, THE STATE

"And I saw," says the apostle John, "three unclean spirits like frogs come out of the mouth of the dragon, and out of the mouth of the beast, and out of the mouth of the false prophet. For they are the spirits of devils, working miracles, which go forth unto the kings of the earth and of the whole world, to gather them to the battle of that great day of God Almighty." Revelation 16:13, 14.

Three deceitful powers unite and require the assistance of the kings of the whole world, that is, the civil powers, to make the final assault upon God, His people, and His truth.

The dragon here is spiritualism. Primarily the dragon represents Satan. Revelation 12:9. But in this particular case prophecy depicts him as working through the medium of spiritualism. And this manifests itself and works through four different channels: paganism (pagan forms of worship and superstition dominated by spiritualism); modern or social spiritualism; the "Christian" spiritualism, which has amalgamated itself with Protestant or Catholic worship by means of miracles and on the basis of the common doctrine of immortality of the soul; and scientific spiritualism, which is practiced in the form of laboratory investigations, under the name of parapsychology or other modern designations.

The beast is the papacy (the first beast of Revelation 13).

The false prophet is the sector of Protestantism which, after hearing the truth, will reject it, uniting to summon the support of the state.

"In chapter 13 (verses 1-10) is described another beast, 'like unto a leopard,' to which the dragon gave 'his power, and his seat, and great authority.' This symbol, as most Protestants have believed, represents the papacy."—GC 439.

" 'And the dragon was wroth with the woman, and went to make war with the remnant of her seed, which keep the commandments of God, and have the testimony of Jesus Christ.' [Revelation 12:17.] In the near future we shall see these words fulfilled as the Protestant churches unite with the world and with the papal power against commandment keepers. The same spirit which actuated papists in ages past will lead Protestants to pursue a similar course toward those who will maintain their loyalty to God.

"Church and state are now making preparations for the future conflict. Protestants are working in disguise to bring Sunday to the front, as did the Romanists."—5T 449 (2TT 149).

"Little by little he [Satan] has prepared the way for his master-piece of deception in the development of spiritualism. He has not yet reached the full accomplishment of his designs; but it will be reached in the last remnant of time. Says the prophet: 'I saw three unclean spirits like frogs; . . . they are the spirits of devils, working miracles, which go forth unto the kings of the earth and of the whole world, to gather them to the battle of that great day of God Almighty.' Revelation 16:13, 14. Except those who are kept by the power of God, through faith in His Word, the whole world will be swept into the ranks of this delusion."—GC 561, 562.

"Protestantism shall give the hand of fellowship to the Roman power. Then there will be a law against the Sabbath of God's creation, and then it is that God will do His 'strange work' in the earth. He has borne long with the perversity of the race; He has tried to win them to Himself. But the time will come when they shall have filled their measure of iniquity; and then it is that God will work. This time is almost reached. God keeps a record with the nations: the figures are swelling against them in the books of heaven; and when it shall have become a law that the transgression of the first day of the week shall be met with punishment, then their cup will be full."—7BC 910.

"When Protestantism shall stretch her hand across the gulf to grasp the hand of the Roman power, when she shall reach over the abyss to clasp hands with spiritualism, when, under the influence of this threefold union, our country shall repudiate every principle of its Constitution as a Protestant and republican government, and shall make provision for the propagation of papal falsehoods and delusions, then we may know that the time has come for the marvelous working of Satan and that the end is near.

"As the approach of the Roman armies was a sign to the disciples of the impending destruction of Jerusalem, so may this apostasy be a sign to us that the limit of God's forbearance is reached, that the measure of our nation's iniquity is full, and that the angel of mercy is about to take her flight, never to return. The people of God will then be plunged into those scenes of affliction and distress which prophets have described as the time of Jacob's trouble."—5T 451 (2TT 150, 151).

"The powers of earth, uniting to war against the commandments of God, will decree that 'all, both small and great, rich and poor, free and bond' (Revelation 13:16), shall conform to the customs of the church by the observance of the false sabbath."—GC 604.

"Through the two great errors, the immortality of the soul and Sunday sacredness, Satan will bring the people under his deceptions. While the former lays the foundation of spiritualism, the latter creates a bond of sympathy with Rome. The Protestants of the United States will be foremost in stretching their hands across the gulf to grasp the hand of spiritualism; they will reach over the abyss to clasp hands with the Roman power; and under the influence of this threefold union, this country will follow in the steps of Rome in trampling on the rights of conscience."—GC 588.

"The professed Protestant world will form a confederacy with the man of sin, and the church and the world will be in corrupt harmony. Here the great crisis is coming upon the world. The Scriptures teach that popery is to regain its lost supremacy, and that the fires of persecution will be rekindled through the time-serving concessions of the so-called Protestant world."—2SM 367, 368.

"Protestant governments will reach a strange pass. They will be converted to the world. They will also, in their separation from God, work to make falsehood and apostasy from God the law of the nation."—RH, June 15, 1897.

"In order for the United States to form an image of the beast, the religious power must so control the civil government that the authority of the state will also be employed by the church to accomplish her own ends."—GC 443.

"Papists, Protestants, and worldlings will alike accept the form of godliness without the power, and they will see in this union a grand movement for the conversion of the world and the ushering in of the long-expected millennium."—GC 588, 589.

"In both the Old and the New World, the papacy will receive homage in the honor paid to the Sunday institution, that rests solely upon the authority of the Roman Church."—GC 579.

"Marvelous in her shrewdness and cunning is the Roman Church. She can read what is to be. She bides her time, seeing that the

Protestant churches are paying her homage in their acceptance of the false sabbath and that they are preparing to enforce it by the very means which she herself employed in bygone days. Those who reject the light of truth will yet seek the aid of this self-styled infallible power to exalt an institution that originated with her. How readily she will come to the help of Protestants in this it is not difficult to conjecture. Who understands better than the papal leaders how to deal with those who are disobedient to the church?

"The Roman Catholic Church, with all its ramifications throughout the world, forms one vast organization under the control, and designed to serve the interests, of the papal see. Its millions of communicants, in every country on the globe, are instructed to hold themselves as bound in allegiance to the pope. Whatever their nationality or their government, they are to regard the authority of the church as above all other. Though they may take the oath pledging their loyalty to the state, yet back of this lies the vow of obedience to Rome, absolving them from every pledge inimical to her interests."—GC 580.

"And let it be remembered, it is the boast of Rome that she never changes. The principles of Gregory VII and Innocent III are still the principles of the Roman Catholic Church. And had she but the power, she would put them in practice with as much vigor now as in past centuries. Protestants little know what they are doing when they propose to accept the aid of Rome in the work of Sunday exaltation. While they are bent upon the accomplishment of their purpose, Rome is aiming to reestablish her power, to recover her lost supremacy. Let the principle once be established in the United States that the church may employ or control the power of the state; that religious observances may be enforced by secular laws; in short, that the authority of church and state is to dominate the conscience, and the triumph of Rome in this country is assured."—GC 581.

"The papal church will never relinquish her claim to infallibility. All that she has done in her persecution of those who reject her dogmas she holds to be right; and would she not repeat the same acts, should the opportunity be presented? Let the restraints now imposed by secular governments be removed and Rome be reinstated in her former power, and there would speedily be a revival of her tyranny and persecution."—GC 564.

"A large class, even of those who look upon Romanism with no favor, apprehend little danger from her power and influence. Many urge that the intellectual and moral darkness prevailing during the

Middle Ages favored the spread of her dogmas, superstitions, and oppression, and that the greater intelligence of modern times, the general diffusion of knowledge, and the increasing liberality in matters of religion forbid a revival of intolerance and tyranny. The very thought that such a state of things will exist in this enlightened age is ridiculed. It is true that great light, intellectual, moral, and religious, is shining upon this generation. In the open pages of God's Holy Word, light from heaven has been shed upon the world. But it should be remembered that the greater the light bestowed, the greater the darkness of those who pervert and reject it."—GC 572.

"The Roman Church now presents a fair front to the world, covering with apologies her record of horrible cruelties. She has clothed herself in Christlike garments; but she is unchanged. Every principle of the papacy that existed in past ages exists today. The doctrines devised in the darkest ages are still held. Let none deceive themselves. The papacy that Protestants are now so ready to honor is the same that ruled the world in the days of the Reformation, when men of God stood up, at the peril of their lives, to expose her iniquity."—GC 571.

"The power attending the message [of the third angel] will only madden those who oppose it. . . . The church appeals to the strong arm of civil power, and, in this work, papists and Protestants unite. As the movement for Sunday enforcement becomes more bold and decided, the law will be invoked against commandment keepers. They will be threatened with fines and imprisonment, and some will be offered positions of influence, and other rewards and advantages, as inducements to renounce their faith."—GC 607.

"Protestantism is now reaching hands across the gulf to clasp hands with the papacy, and a confederacy is being formed to trample out of sight the Sabbath of the fourth commandment; and the man of sin, who, at the instigation of Satan, instituted the spurious sabbath—this child of the papacy—will be exalted to take the place of God."—*An Appeal to Ministers and Conference Committees*, page 38. Printed by the General Conference in 1892.

THE IMAGE TO THE BEAST

"Saying [the beast with horns like a lamb, that is, the United States] to them that dwell on the earth, that they should make an image to the beast, which had the wound by a sword, and did live. And he had power to give life unto the image of the beast." Revelation 13:14, 15.

Here the beast with horns like a lamb (the United States) orders the inhabitants of the land to erect an image to the Roman beast, and also to infuse breath and life into this image.

If the beast (the power symbolized in Revelation 13:1-10, that is, papal Rome) is an ecclesiastical-political persecuting power and the enemy of God, the *image of the beast* must be something similar.

The fact that the United States orders its inhabitants to form an image of the beast indicates that its government, in cooperation with ecclesiastical authorities, will also force the minority to conform in religious matters, in this case in the observance of Sunday.

Just as the first beast of Revelation 13 sought the aid of civil power to persecute "heretics," the image of the beast will do the same.

The image of the beast, then, represents apostate Protestantism united with the state in a confederacy to enforce its religious dogmas, particularly Sunday.

"The 'image to the beast' represents that form of apostate Protestantism which will be developed when the Protestant churches shall seek the aid of the civil power for the enforcement of their dogmas." —GC 445.

"Only by changing God's law could the papacy exalt itself above God; whoever should understandingly keep the law as thus changed would be giving supreme honor to that power by which the change was made. Such an act of obedience to papal laws would be a mark of allegiance to the pope in the place of God."—GC 446.

"In order for the United States to form an image of the beast, the religious power must so control the civil government that the authority of the state will also be employed by the church to accomplish her own ends."—GC 443.

"When the leading churches of the United States, uniting upon such points of doctrine as are held by them in common, shall influence the state to enforce their decrees and to sustain their institutions, then Protestant America will have formed an image of the Roman hierarchy, and the infliction of civil penalties upon dissenters will inevitably result."—GC 445.

"The enforcement of Sunday keeping on the part of Protestant churches is an enforcement of the worship of the papacy—of the beast. Those who, understanding the claims of the fourth commandment, choose to observe the false instead of the true Sabbath are thereby paying homage to that power by which alone it is commanded. But in the very act of enforcing religious duty by secular power, the churches would themselves form an image to the beast; hence the enforcement of Sunday keeping in the United States would be an enforcement of the worship of the beast and his image."—GC 448, 449.

THE MARK OF THE BEAST

"And he [the beast with horns like a lamb, that is, the United States] causeth all, both small and great, rich and poor, free and bond, to receive a mark in their right hand, or in their foreheads: and that no man might buy or sell, save he that had the mark, or the name of the beast, or the number of his name." Revelation 13:16, 17.

Although we do not yet understand all that is involved in the mark of the beast, we do know that the mark will designate those who observe Sunday. But this will occur only when they have rejected fully the Sabbath truth at the time Sunday is enforced by law.

It is the beast with horns like a lamb (that is, the United States), the power which at the urging of the apostate Protestant confederation makes an image of the beast, which imposes the mark of the first beast, that is, Rome. It is the state which impresses religious observance of Sunday by coercive legislation and makes that observance compulsory, persecuting those who oppose it. At first it will be the United States which imposes this observance, but very soon the other countries around the world will do the same.

God accepts the sincerity of those who innocently observe Sunday, believing it to be the true day of worship. The mark of the beast will be placed on them only when they know the teaching of the Bible in favor of Sabbath and are in a position to make an intelligent decision between truth and error. This will be when Sunday observance is enforced by law in the United States and around the world.

Those who reject the mark of the beast and demonstrate their loyalty to God by the observance of Sabbath, thus receiving the seal of the living God, will be denied their most fundamental rights, such as to buy, sell, work, et cetera. But the Lord will be their all-powerful help and protection.

"The sign, or seal, of God is revealed in the observance of the seventh-day Sabbath, the Lord's memorial of creation. 'The Lord spake unto Moses, saying, Speak thou also unto the children of Israel, saying, Verily My Sabbaths ye shall keep: for it is a sign between Me and you throughout your generations; that ye may know that I am the Lord that doth sanctify you.' Exodus 31:12, 13. Here the Sabbath is clearly designated as a sign between God and His people.

"The mark of the beast is the opposite of this—the observance of the first day of the week. This mark distinguishes those who acknowledge the supremacy of the papal authority from those who acknowledge the authority of God."—8T 117 (3TT 232).

Commenting on Revelation 14:9-12, Mrs. White declares:

"John was called to behold a people distinct from those who worship the beast or his image by keeping the first day of the week. The observance of this day is the mark of the beast."—TM 133.

"The light we have received upon the third angel's message is the true light. The mark of the beast is exactly what it has been proclaimed to be. Not all in regard to this matter is yet understood, nor will it be understood until the unrolling of the scroll; but a most solemn work is to be accomplished in our world."—6T 17 (2TT 371).

"The Sabbath will be the great test of loyalty, for it is the point of truth especially controverted. When the final test shall be brought to bear upon men, then the line of distinction will be drawn between those who serve God and those who serve Him not. While the observance of the false sabbath in compliance with the law of the state, contrary to the fourth commandment, will be an avowal of allegiance to a power that is in opposition to God, the keeping of the true Sabbath, in obedience to God's law, is an evidence of loyalty to the Creator. While one class, by accepting the sign of submission to earthly powers, receive the mark of the beast, the other, choosing the token of allegiance to divine authority, receive the seal of God."—GC 605.

"As men then reject the institution which God has declared to be the sign of His authority, and honor in its stead that which Rome has chosen as the token of her supremacy, they will thereby accept the sign of allegiance to Rome—'the mark of the beast.' "—GC 449.

"During the Christian dispensation, the great enemy of man's happiness has made the Sabbath of the fourth commandment an object of special attack. Satan says, 'I will work at cross purposes with God. I will empower my followers to set aside God's memorial, the seventh-day Sabbath. Thus I will show the world that the day sanctified and blessed by God has been changed. That day shall not live in the minds of the people. I will obliterate the memory of it. I will place in its stead a day that does not bear the credentials of God, a day that cannot be a sign between God and His people. I will lead those who accept this day to place upon it the sanctity that God placed upon the seventh day. . . .

" 'Human laws will be made so stringent that men and women will not dare to observe the seventh-day Sabbath. For fear of wanting food and clothing, they will join with the world in transgressing God's law. The earth will be wholly under my [Satan's] dominion.' " —PK 183, 184.

"To secure popularity and patronage, legislators will yield to the demand for a Sunday law. Those who fear God cannot accept an institution that violates a precept of the Decalogue."—5T 451.

"Christians of past generations observed the Sunday, supposing that in so doing they were keeping the Bible Sabbath; and there are now true Christians in every church, not excepting the Roman Catholic communion, who honestly believe that Sunday is the Sabbath of divine appointment. God accepts their sincerity of purpose and their integrity before Him. But when Sunday observance shall be enforced by law, and the world shall be enlightened concerning the obligation of the true Sabbath, then whoever shall transgress the command of God, to obey a precept which has no higher authority than that of Rome, will thereby honor popery above God. He is paying homage to Rome and to the power which enforces the institution ordained by Rome. He is worshiping the beast and his image. As men then reject the institution which God has declared to be the sign of His authority, and honor in its stead that which Rome has chosen as the token of her supremacy, they will thereby accept the sign of allegiance to Rome—'the mark of the beast.' And it is not until the issue is thus plainly set before the people, and they are brought to choose between the commandments of God and the commandments of men, that those who continue in transgression will receive 'the mark of the beast.' "—GC 449.

"All who refuse compliance will be visited with civil penalties, and it will finally be declared that they are deserving of death. On the other hand, the law of God enjoining the Creator's rest day demands obedience and threatens wrath against all who transgress its precepts.

"With the issue thus clearly brought before him, whoever shall trample upon God's law to obey a human enactment receives the mark of the beast; he accepts the sign of allegiance to the power which he chooses to obey instead of God."—GC 604.

SUNDAY LAWS

On May 29, 1961, the Supreme Court of the United States, by a majority vote, handed down a decision of historic importance, particularly from the prophetic point of view. It declared that Sunday laws are civil, not religious, in nature, and therefore are constitutional. This decision threw wide open the doors for further enactment of Sunday legislation in all the states of the country.

At present most of the states have Sunday laws in some form, in many cases with limited application.

Now a movement is on foot to revise these laws and make them stricter and more inclusive. This has opened the way for a more complete fulfillment of prophecy.

We shall not further expand on this aspect, but the reader is directed to the Appendix, where a series of prophetic facts of great significance on this vital theme is presented.

SUNDAY AS A DAY OF MISSIONARY WORK

"When we devote Sunday to missionary work, the whip will be taken out of the hands of the arbitrary zealots who would be well pleased to humiliate Seventh-day Adventists. When they see that we employ ourselves on Sunday in visiting the people and opening the Scriptures to them, they will know that it is useless for them to try to hinder our work by making Sunday laws."—9T 232, 233 (3TT 395).

"Dear Brother: I will try to answer your question as to what you should do in the case of Sunday laws being enforced.

"The light given me by the Lord at a time when we were expecting just such a crisis as you seem to be approaching, was that when the people were moved by a power from beneath to enforce Sunday observance, Seventh-day Adventists were to show their wisdom by refraining from their ordinary work on that day, devoting it to missionary effort.

"To defy the Sunday laws will but strengthen in their persecution the religious zealots who are seeking to enforce them. Give them no occasion to call you lawbreakers. If they are left to rein up men who fear neither God nor man, the reining up will soon lose its novelty for them, and they will see that it is not consistent nor convenient for them to be strict in regard to the observance of the Sunday. Keep right on with your missionary work, with your Bibles in your hands, and the enemy will see that he has worsted his own cause. One does not receive the mark of the beast because he shows that he realizes the wisdom of keeping the peace by refraining from work that gives offense, doing at the same time a work of the highest importance." —9T 232 (3TT 395).

"Let the teachers in our schools devote Sunday to missionary effort. I was instructed that they would thus be able to defeat the purposes of the enemy. Let the teachers take the students with them to hold meetings for those who know not the truth. Thus they will accomplish much more than they could in any other way."—9T 233 (3TT 396).

"Employ Sunday in doing missionary work for God. Teachers, go with your students. Take them into the bush [this is what we called the sparsely settled districts in the woods, where houses are often a mile or two apart], and visit the people in their homes."—9T 237 (3TT 400).

ONLY TWO CLASSES

When the great crisis comes upon the church, Christianity will be divided into two distinct groups: those loyal to God's commandments, including the Sabbath commandment, and those who are enemies of truth and keep Sunday. The first, the minority, will be despised and persecuted by the majority.

"The wicked will be distinguished by their efforts to tear down the Creator's memorial and to exalt the institution of Rome. In the issue of the conflict all Christendom will be divided into two great classes, those who keep the commandments of God and the faith of Jesus, and those who worship the beast and his image, and receive his mark. Although church and state will unite their power to compel all, 'both small and great, rich and poor, free and bond,' to receive the mark of the beast, yet the people of God will not receive it."—9T 16, 17 (3TT 285).

"In the issue of the contest all Christendom will be divided into two great classes—those who keep the commandments of God and the faith of Jesus, and those who worship the beast and his image and receive his mark."—GC 450.

"The enmity of Satan against good will be manifested more and more as he brings his forces into activity in his last work of rebellion; and every soul that is not fully surrendered to God, and kept by divine power, will form an alliance with Satan against heaven, and join in battle against the Ruler of the universe."—TM 465.

"The warfare against God's law, which was begun in heaven, will be continued until the end of time. Every man will be tested. Obedience or disobedience is the question to be decided by the whole world. All will be called to choose between the law of God and the laws of men. Here the dividing line will be drawn. There will be but two classes. Every character will be fully developed; and all will show whether they have chosen the side of loyalty or that of rebellion. "Then the end will come."—DA 763.

"But when the world makes void the law of God, what will be the effect upon the truly obedient and righteous? Will they be carried away by the strong current of evil? Because so many rank themselves under the banner of the prince of darkness, will God's commandment-keeping people swerve from their allegiance? Never! Not one who is abiding in Christ will fail or fall. His followers will bow in obedience to a higher authority than that of any earthly potentate. While the contempt placed upon God's commandments leads many to suppress the truth and show less reverence for it, the faithful ones will with greater earnestness hold aloft its distinguishing truth."— 2SM 368, 369.

THE DEATH DECREE

"And he [the beast with horns like a lamb, that is, the United States] had power to give life to the image of the beast [that is, apostate Protestantism united with the state], that the image of the beast should both speak, and cause that as many as would not worship the image of the beast should be killed." Revelation 13:15.

This decree of death will be promulgated after the close of probation, during the great time of trouble, and will cause the flight of the children of God from the small cities (they will already have left the large cities when the Sunday law was pronounced). An exact time will be set for the decree to go into effect.

But, thank God, none of the faithful will be destroyed. During the time that will intervene before the hour set for destruction, God will miraculously protect His chosen ones, those who are sealed. And at the precise instant of the expiration of the time, tremendous supernatural upheavals will occur, which will paralyze the wicked and deliver the righteous. (See chapters 10 and 11 of this volume under the seventh plague for a more complete presentation of these events.)

"The powers of earth, uniting to war against the commandments of God, will decree that 'all, both small and great, rich and poor, free and bond' (Revelation 13:16), shall conform to the customs of the church by the observance of the false sabbath. All who refuse compliance will be visited with civil penalties, and it will finally be declared that they are deserving of death."—GC 604.

"The decree will go forth that they must disregard the Sabbath of the fourth commandment, and honor the first day, or lose their lives."—1T 353, 354 (1TT 131).

"I saw that the four angels would hold the four winds until Jesus' work was done in the sanctuary, and then will come the seven last plagues. These plagues enraged the wicked against the righteous; they thought that we had brought the judgments of God upon them, and that if they could rid the earth of us, the plagues would then be stayed. A decree went forth to slay the saints, which caused them to cry day and night for deliverance. This was the time of Jacob's trouble."—EW 36, 37.

"Especially will the wrath of man be aroused against those who hallow the Sabbath of the fourth commandment; and at last a universal decree will denounce these as deserving of death."—PK 512.

"When the protection of human laws shall be withdrawn from those who honor the law of God, there will be, in different lands, a simultaneous movement for their destruction. As the time appointed in the decree draws near, the people will conspire to root out the hated sect. It will be determined to strike in one night a decisive blow, which shall utterly silence the voice of dissent and reproof."—GC 635.

It is said here that the death decree will be put into effect at night. Since according to civil law the legal day starts at midnight, it is understandable how this hour would be set for the execution of this decree. Later we shall observe also that it will be at midnight when God delivers His people.

A certain period of time will elapse between the promulgation of the decree and the date of its execution. We do not know how long this will be.

"The heavenly sentinels, faithful to their trust, continue their watch. Though a general decree has fixed the time when commandment keepers may be put to death, their enemies will in some cases anticipate the decree, and before the time specified, will endeavor to take their lives. But none can pass the mighty guardians stationed about every faithful soul. Some are assailed in their flight from the cities and villages; but the swords raised against them break and fall powerless as a straw. Others are defended by angels in the form of men of war."—GC 631.

"The decree which is to go forth against the people of God will be very similar to that issued by Ahasuerus against the Jews in the time of Esther."—5T 450 (2TT 149).

"As the decree issued by the various rulers of Christendom against the commandment keepers shall withdraw the protection of government and abandon them to those who desire their destruction, the people of God will flee from the cities and villages and associate together in companies, dwelling in the most desolate and solitary places. Many will find refuge in the strongholds of the mountains."—GC 626.

LEAVING THE CITIES

God has graciously given advance warning to Seventh-day Adventists of the perplexing times which await the church, especially when a decree will be passed excluding Sabbath keepers from purchasing the necessities of life. Many families, as the Lord opens the way, will in advance of the crisis leave the cities and locate in a rural environment conducive to physical and spiritual welfare, and suitable for growing some of the family food supply.

"We are not to locate ourselves where we will be forced into close relations with those who do not honor God. . . . A crisis is soon to come in regard to the observance of Sunday. . . .

"The Sunday party is strengthening itself in its false claims, and this will mean oppression to those who determine to keep the Sabbath of the Lord. We are to place ourselves where we can carry out the Sabbath commandment in its fullness. . . . And we are to be careful not to place ourselves where it will be hard for ourselves and our children to keep the Sabbath.

"If in the providence of God we can secure places away from the cities, the Lord would have us do this. There are troublous times before us.

"When the power invested in kings is allied to goodness, it is because the one in responsibility is under the divine dictation. When power is allied with wickedness, it is allied to Satanic agencies, and it will work to destroy those who are the Lord's property. The Protestant world have set up an idol sabbath in the place where God's Sabbath should be, and they are treading in the footsteps of the papacy. For this reason I see the necessity of the people of God moving out of the cities into retired country [places], where they may cultivate the land and raise their own produce. Thus they may bring their children up with simple, healthful habits. I see the necessity of making haste to get all things ready for the crisis."—2SM 359.

"The time is fast coming when the controlling power of the labor unions will be very oppressive. Again and again the Lord has instructed that our people are to take their families away from the cities, into the country, where they can raise their own provisions; for in the future the problem of buying and selling will be a very serious one. We should now begin to heed the instruction given us over and over again: Get out of the cities into rural districts, where the houses are not crowded closely together, and where you will be free from the interference of enemies."—2SM 141.

EMERGENCY FLIGHT FROM THE CITIES

When the Sunday law is passed and strictly enforced, it will be time for the faithful to leave the large cities. This will have to be done quickly.

After the close of probation, while the plagues are being poured out and when the death decree is promulgated, the children of God will flee from the small cities, the villages, and the populated areas.

"It is no time now for God's people to be fixing their affections or laying up their treasure in the world. The time is not far distant, when, like the early disciples, we shall be forced to seek a refuge in desolate and solitary places. As the siege of Jerusalem by the Roman armies was the signal for flight to the Judean Christians, so the assumption of power on the part of our nation [the United States] in the decree enforcing the papal sabbath will be a warning to us. It will then be time to leave the large cities, preparatory to leaving the smaller ones for retired homes in secluded places among the mountains."—5T 464, 465 (2TT 166).

"As the decree issued by the various rulers of Christendom against commandment keepers shall withdraw the protection of government and abandon them to those who desire their destruction, the people of God will flee from the cities and villages and associate together in companies, dwelling in the most desolate and solitary places. Many will find refuge in the strongholds of the mountains. . . . But many of all nations and of all classes, high and low, rich and poor, black and white, will be cast into the most unjust and cruel bondage. The beloved of God pass weary days, bound in chains, shut in by prison bars, sentenced to be slain, some apparently left to die of starvation in dark and loathsome dungeons. No human ear is open to hear their moans; no human hand is ready to lend them help. . . .

"Though enemies may thrust them into prison, yet dungeon walls cannot cut off the communication between their souls and Christ. One who sees their every weakness, who is acquainted with every trial, is above all earthly powers; and angels will come to them in lonely cells, bringing light and peace from heaven."—GC 626, 627.

"I saw the saints leaving the cities and villages, and associating together in companies, and living in the most solitary places. Angels provided them food and water, while the wicked were suffering from hunger and thirst."—EW 282.

THE SONG OF VICTORY

Thanks be to God for the prophetic picture He has inspired Bible writers and His latter-day messenger to paint. We see the "little flock"—the saints who bear the seal of God, who have kept their faith, and who have passed unharmed through the hour of trial under the marvelous protection of the Most High. They are portrayed standing at last on the sea of glass singing the song of victory. Says the prophet: "And I saw as it were a sea of glass mingled with fire: and them that had gotten the victory over the beast, and over his image, and over his mark, and over the number of his name, stand on the sea of glass, having the harps of God. And they sing the song of Moses the servant of God, and the song of the Lamb." Revelation 15:2, 3.

CHAPTER 7

THE WORK OF DECEPTION: SPIRITUALISM

Synthesis—Deceitful miracles—Satanic delusions—Attempt to imitate the second coming of Christ—A defense against deceptions—Safeguard against spiritualism.

SYNTHESIS

THE LAST DAYS will be characterized by an extraordinary manifestation of spiritualism. It will emerge as one of the three great powers to deceive and persecute the faithful. Spiritualism not only appears as a member of the terrible triple alliance mentioned in Revelation 16:13, 14—there called "the dragon"—but it also acts as the common medium for binding the other members together.

Therefore after the prophet says that he saw three unclean spirits come out of the mouth of the dragon (spiritualism), the beast (Catholicism), and the false prophet (apostate Protestantism), he adds that the three are "spirits of devils, working miracles." In other words, spiritualism dominates the three institutions, and it will manifest itself by means of supernatural works.

This process will culminate in Satan's attempt to imitate time's greatest event—the second coming of Christ.

The only way anyone can be protected from these deceptions —ever more subtle as time advances—is to be firmly rooted in the truth by the study of the Word of God and the spirit of prophecy.

DECEITFUL MIRACLES

"And I saw three unclean spirits like frogs come out of the mouth of the dragon, and out of the mouth of the beast, and out of the mouth of the false prophet. For they are the spirits of devils, working miracles, which go forth unto the kings of the earth and of the whole world, to gather them to the battle of that great day of God Almighty." Revelation 16:13, 14.

"For there shall arise false christs, and false prophets, and shall show great signs and wonders; insomuch that, if it were possible, they shall deceive the very elect." Matthew 24:24.

"And he doeth great wonders, so that he maketh fire come down from heaven on the earth in the sight of men, and deceiveth them that dwell on the earth by the means of those miracles which he had power to do in the sight of the beast; saying to them that dwell on the earth, that they should make an image to the beast, which had the wound by a sword, and did live." Revelation 13:13, 14.

"I saw that soon* it would be considered blasphemy to speak against the rapping, and that it would spread more and more, that Satan's power would increase, and some of his devoted followers would have power to work miracles, and even to bring down fire from heaven in the sight of men. I was shown that by the rapping and mesmerism these modern magicians would yet account for all the miracles wrought by our Lord Jesus Christ, and that many would believe that all the mighty works of the Son of God when on earth were accomplished by this same power."—EW 86, 87.

"The Protestants of the United States will be foremost in stretching their hands across the gulf to grasp the hand of spiritualism; they will reach over the abyss to clasp hands with the Roman power; and under the influence of this threefold union, this country will follow in the steps of Rome in trampling on the rights of conscience.

"As spiritualism more closely imitates the nominal Christianity of the day, it has greater power to deceive and ensnare. Satan himself is converted, after the modern order of things. He will appear in the character of an angel of light. Through the agency of spiritualism, miracles will be wrought, the sick will be healed, and many undeniable wonders will be performed. And as the spirits will profess faith in the Bible, and manifest respect for the institutions of the church, their work will be accepted as a manifestation of divine power."— GC 588.

"While appearing to the children of men as a great physician who can heal all their maladies, he will bring disease and disaster, until populous cities are reduced to ruin and desolation."—GC 589.

"Satan works through the elements also to garner his harvest of

*Written August 24, 1850.

unprepared souls. He has studied the secrets of the laboratories of nature, and he uses all his power to control the elements as far as God allows."—GC 589.

"Satan also works with lying wonders, even bringing down fire from heaven in the sight of men. Revelation 13:13. Thus the inhabitants of the earth will be brought to take their stand."—GC 612.

"Side by side with the preaching of the gospel, agencies are at work which are but the medium of lying spirits. Many a man tampers with these merely from curiosity, but seeing evidence of the working of a more than human power, he is lured on and on, until he is controlled by a will stronger than his own. He cannot escape from its mysterious power."—DA 258.

"The line of distinction between professed Christians and the ungodly is now hardly distinguishable. Church members love what the world loves and are ready to join with them, and Satan determines to unite them in one body and thus strengthen his cause by sweeping all into the ranks of spiritualism. Papists, who boast of miracles as a certain sign of the true church, will be readily deceived by this wonder-working power; and Protestants, having cast away the shield of truth, will also be deluded. Papists, Protestants, and worldlings will alike accept the form of godliness without the power, and they will see in this union a grand movement for the conversion of the world and the ushering in of the long-expected millennium.

"Through spiritualism, Satan appears as a benefactor of the race, healing the diseases of the people, and professing to present a new and more exalted system of religious faith; but at the same time he works as a destroyer. His temptations are leading multitudes to ruin. Intemperance dethrones reason; sensual indulgence, strife, and bloodshed follow. Satan delights in war, for it excites the worst passions of the soul and then sweeps into eternity its victims steeped in vice and blood. It is his object to incite the nations to war against one another, for he can thus divert the minds of the people from the work of preparation to stand in the day of God."—GC 588, 589.

"In accidents and calamities by sea and by land, in great conflagrations, in fierce tornadoes and terrific hailstorms, in tempests, floods, cyclones, tidal waves, and earthquakes, in every place and in a thousand forms, Satan is exercising his power. He sweeps away the ripening harvest, and famine and distress follow. He imparts to the air a deadly taint, and thousands perish by the pestilence. These visitations are to become more and more frequent and disastrous. Destruction will be upon both man and beast. 'The earth mourneth and fadeth away,' 'the haughty people . . . do languish. The earth also is defiled under the inhabitants thereof; because they have transgressed the laws, changed the ordinance, broken the everlasting covenant.' Isaiah 24:4, 5."—GC 589, 590.

"The last great delusion is soon to open before us. Antichrist is to perform his marvelous works in our sight. So closely will the counterfeit resemble the true that it will be impossible to distinguish between them except by the Holy Scriptures."—GC 593.

"Soon the battle will be waged fiercely between those who serve God and those who serve Him not. Soon everything that can be shaken will be shaken, that those things that cannot be shaken may remain. . . .

"And Satan, surrounded by evil angels, and claiming to be God, will work miracles of all kinds, to deceive, if possible, the very elect. . . . God's tried and tested people will find their power in the sign spoken of in Exodus 31:12-18. They are to take their stand on the living word: 'It is written.' This is the only foundation upon which they can stand securely. Those who have broken their covenant with God will in that day be without God and without hope."—9T 15, 16 (3TT 284, 285).

SATANIC DELUSIONS

"Even him, whose coming is after the working of Satan with all power and signs and lying wonders, and with all deceivableness of unrighteousness in them that perish; because they received not the love of the truth, that they might be saved. And for this cause God shall send them strong delusion, that they should believe a lie." 2 Thessalonians 2:9-11.

"Through the two great errors, the immortality of the soul and Sunday sacredness, Satan will bring the people under his deceptions."—GC 588.

"That time will soon come, and we shall have to keep hold of the strong arm of Jehovah; for all these great signs and mighty wonders of the devil are designed to deceive God's people and overthrow them."—EW 60.

"A belief in spiritual manifestations opens the door to seducing spirits and doctrines of devils, and thus the influence of evil angels will be felt in the churches."—GC 604.

"Communications from the spirits will declare that God has sent them to convince the rejecters of Sunday of their error, affirming that the laws of the land should be obeyed as the law of God. They will lament the great wickedness in the world and second the testimony of religious teachers that the degraded state of morals is caused by the desecration of Sunday. Great will be the indignation excited against all who refuse to accept their testimony.".—GC 591.

"Love is dwelt upon as the chief attribute of God, but it is degraded to a weak sentimentalism, making little distinction between good and evil. God's justice, His denunciations of sin, the requirements of His holy law, are all kept out of sight. The people are taught to regard the Decalogue as a dead letter. Pleasing, bewitching fables captivate the senses and lead men to reject the Bible as the foundation of their faith. Christ is as verily denied as before; but Satan has so blinded the eyes of the people that the deception is not discerned.".—GC 558.

"We have reached the perils of the last days, when some, yes, many, shall depart from the faith, giving heed to seducing spirits and doctrines of devils. Be cautious in regard to what you read and how you hear. Take not a particle of interest in spiritualistic theories. Satan is waiting to steal a march upon everyone who allows himself to be deceived by his hypnotism. He begins to exert his power over them just as soon as they begin to investigate his theories." —MM 101, 102.

"Satan has long been preparing for his final effort to deceive the world. The foundation of his work was laid by the assurance given to Eve in Eden: 'Ye shall not surely die.' 'In the day ye eat thereof, then your eyes shall be opened, and ye shall be as gods, knowing good and evil.' Genesis 3:4, 5. Little by little he has prepared the way for his masterpiece of deception in the development of spiritualism. He has not yet reached the full accomplishment of his designs; but it will be reached in the last remnant of time. Says the prophet: 'I saw three unclean spirits like frogs; . . . they are the spirits of devils, working miracles, which go forth unto the kings of the earth and of the whole world, to gather them to the battle of that great day of God Almighty.' Revelation 16:13, 14.".—GC 561, 562.

"The apostles, as personated by these lying spirits, are made to contradict what they wrote at the dictation of the Holy Spirit when on earth.".—GC 557.

"At the same time there will be a power working from beneath. While God's agents of mercy work through consecrated human beings, Satan sets his agencies in operation, laying under tribute all who will submit to his control. There will be lords many and gods many. The cry will be heard, 'Lo, here is Christ,' and, 'Lo, there is Christ.' The deep plotting of Satan will reveal itself everywhere for the purpose of diverting the attention of men and women from present duty. There will be signs and wonders. But the eye of faith will discern in all these manifestations harbingers of the grand and awful future, and the triumphs that await the people of God."— 9T 47.

"Even in its present form, so far from being more worthy of toleration than formerly, it is really a more dangerous, because a more subtle, deception. While it formerly denounced Christ and the Bible, it now *professes* to accept both. But the Bible is interpreted in a manner that is pleasing to the unrenewed heart, while its solemn and vital truths are made of no effect."—GC 558.

"Many will be ensnared through the belief that spiritualism is a merely human imposture; when brought face to face with manifestations which they cannot but regard as supernatural, they will be deceived, and will be led to accept them as the great power of God." —GC 553.

"As we near the close of time, there will be greater and still greater external parade of heathen power; heathen deities will manifest their signal power, and will exhibit themselves before the cities of the world; and this delineation has already begun to be fulfilled."—TM 117, 118.

"So it will be in the great final conflict of the controversy between righteousness and sin. While new life and light and power are descending from on high upon the disciples of Christ, a new life is springing up from beneath, and energizing the agencies of Satan. Intensity is taking possession of every earthly element. With a subtlety gained through centuries of conflict, the prince of evil works under a disguise. He appears clothed as an angel of light, and multitudes are 'giving heed to seducing spirits, and doctrines of devils.' 1 Timothy 4:1."—DA 257.

"The prince of darkness, who has so long bent the power of his mastermind to the work of deception, skillfully adapts his temptations to men of all classes and conditions. To persons of culture and refinement he presents spiritualism in its more refined and intellectual aspects, and thus succeeds in drawing many into his snare. The wisdom which spiritualism imparts is that described by the apostle James, which 'descendeth not from above, but is earthly, sensual, devilish.' James 3:15. This, however, the great deceiver conceals when concealment will best suit his purpose. He who could appear clothed with the brightness of the heavenly seraphs before Christ in the wilderness of temptation, comes to men in the most attractive manner as an angel of light. He appeals to the reason by the presentation of elevating themes; he delights the fancy with enrapturing scenes; and he enlists the affections by his eloquent portrayals of love and charity. He excites the imagination to lofty flights, leading men to take so great pride in their own wisdom that in their hearts they despise the Eternal One."—GC 553, 554.

"Fearful sights of a supernatural character will soon be revealed in the heavens, in token of the power of miracle-working demons. The spirits of devils will go forth to the kings of the earth and to the whole world, to fasten them in deception, and urge them on to unite with Satan in his last struggle against the government of heaven. By these agencies, rulers and subjects will be alike deceived. Persons will arise pretending to be Christ Himself, and claiming the title and worship which belong to the world's Redeemer. They will perform wonderful miracles of healing and will profess to have revelations from heaven contradicting the testimony of the Scriptures."—GC 624.

ATTEMPT TO IMITATE THE SECOND COMING OF CHRIST

"And no marvel; for Satan himself is transformed into an angel of light. Therefore it is no great thing if his ministers also be transformed as the ministers of righteousness; whose end shall be according to their works." 2 Corinthians 11:14, 15.

"And then shall that wicked be revealed, whom the Lord shall consume with the spirit of His mouth, and shall destroy with the brightness of His coming: even him, whose coming is after the working of Satan with all power and signs and lying wonders, and with all deceivableness of unrighteousness in them that perish; because they received not the love of the truth, that they might be saved. And for this cause God shall send them strong delusion, that they should believe a lie: that they all might be damned who believed not the truth, but had pleasure in unrighteousness." 2 Thessalonians 2:8-12.

"As the crowning act in the great drama of deception, Satan himself will personate Christ. The church has long professed to look to the Saviour's advent as the consummation of her hopes. Now the great deceiver will make it appear that Christ has come. In different parts of the earth, Satan will manifest himself among men as a majestic being of dazzling brightness, resembling the description of the Son of God given by John in the Revelation. Revelation 1:13-15. The glory that surrounds him is unsurpassed by anything that mortal eyes have yet beheld. The shout of triumph rings out upon the air: 'Christ has come! Christ has come!' The people prostrate themselves in adoration before him, while he lifts up his hands and pronounces a blessing upon them, as Christ blessed His disciples when He was upon the earth. His voice is soft and subdued, yet full of melody. In gentle, compassionate tones he presents some of the same gracious, heavenly truths which the Saviour uttered; he heals the diseases of the people, and then, in his assumed character of Christ, he claims to have changed the Sabbath to Sunday, and commands all to hallow the day which he has blessed. He declares that those who persist in keeping holy the seventh day are blaspheming his name by refusing to listen to his angels sent to them with light and truth. This is the strong, almost overmastering delusion."—GC 624.

"Satan will take the field and personate Christ. He will misrepresent, misapply, and pervert everything he possibly can, to deceive, if possible, the very elect. Even in our day there have been and will continue to be entire families who have once rejoiced in the truth, but who will lose faith because of calumnies and falsehoods brought to them in regard to those whom they have loved and with whom they have had sweet counsel."—TM 411.

"You know that Satan will come in to deceive if possible the very elect. He claims to be Christ, and he is coming in, pretending to be the great medical missionary. He will cause fire to come down from heaven in the sight of men, to prove that he is God. We must stand barricaded by the truths of the Bible."—SpT, Series B, No. 6, p. 33.

"Satan will not only appear as a human being, but he will personate Jesus Christ; and the world that has rejected the truth will receive him as the Lord of lords and King of kings."—5BC 1106.

A DEFENSE AGAINST DECEPTIONS

"Except those who are kept by the power of God, through faith in His Word, the whole world will be swept into the ranks of this delusion. The people are fast being lulled to a fatal security, to be awakened only by the outpouring of the wrath of God."—GC 562.

"The time is at hand when Satan will work miracles to confirm minds in the belief that he is God. . . . All the pleasant pictures, all the miracles wrought, will be presented in order that, if possible, the very elect shall be deceived. The only hope for anyone is to hold fast the evidences that have confirmed the truth in righteousness. Let these be proclaimed over and over again, until the close of this earth's history."—*Medical Ministry*, pages 14, 15.

"But the people of God will not be misled. The teachings of this false christ are not in accordance with the Scriptures. His blessing is pronounced upon the worshipers of the beast and his image, the very class upon whom the Bible declares that God's unmingled wrath shall be poured out. . . .

"Only those who have been diligent students of the Scriptures and who have received the love of the truth will be shielded from the powerful delusion that takes the world captive."—GC 625.

SAFEGUARD AGAINST SPIRITUALISM

"There are few who have any just conception of the deceptive power of spiritualism and the danger of coming under its influence. . . . They venture upon the forbidden ground, and the mighty destroyer exercises his power upon them against their will. Let them once be induced to submit their minds to his direction, and he holds them captive. It is impossible, in their own strength, to break away from the bewitching, alluring spell. Nothing but the power of God, granted in answer to the earnest prayer of faith, can deliver these ensnared souls."—GC 558.

"God's Word, rightly understood and applied, is a safeguard against spiritualism. . . . The Word of God is plain. It is a straight chain of truth, and will prove an anchor to those who are willing to receive it, even if they have to sacrifice their cherished fables. It will save them from the terrible delusions of these perilous times."—1T 344, 345, (1TT 119, 120).

CHAPTER 8

THE EARLY TIME OF TROUBLE

THE ONLY reason for treating this topic in a separate chapter is to help the reader not to fall into any possible confusion with respect to the expression "the time of trouble." In Mrs. White's writings this phrase, "the time of trouble," is applied to two periods of time fundamentally distinct in their characteristics, although both will bring general trouble to the world:

A. *The time that ends at the close of probation.* The Lord referred to this period in His prophetic sermon when He said: "And there shall be . . . upon the earth distress of nations, with perplexity; the sea and the waves roaring; men's hearts failing them for fear, and for looking after those things which are coming on the earth." Luke 21:25, 26.

This period will be characterized by wars, earthquakes, pestilences, false prophets, increasing immorality, signs in the heavens, general fear and apprehension, and the preaching of the gospel in all the world.

It will end at the moment when the decree of Revelation 22:11 is pronounced—or it might be said to merge into the greater time of trouble.

At the very moment of the decree, probation will close.

B. *The time which immediately follows the close of probation* and which ends at the appearance of Christ in the clouds of heaven at His second coming.

. . . . .

For the purpose of making an easy and logical differentiation between the two periods without any possible misunderstanding, we shall designate them in this book as follows:

1. The first period—The early time of trouble.
2. The second period—The time of trouble.

In this connection we insert three paragraphs in which Ellen G. White referred to the early time of trouble and made a distinction between the two periods:

"I saw that God had children who do not see and keep the Sabbath. They have not rejected the light upon it. And at the commencement of the time of trouble, we were filled with the Holy Ghost as we went forth and proclaimed the Sabbath more fully. . . . I saw the sword, famine, pestilence, and great confusion in the land."—EW 33, 34.

" 'The commencement of that time of trouble,' here mentioned [referring to the above-mentioned quotation], does not refer to the time when the plagues shall begin to be poured out, but to a short period just before they are poured out, while Christ is in the sanctuary."—EW 85.

"At that time, while the work of salvation is closing, trouble will be coming on the earth, and the nations will be angry, yet held in check so as not to prevent the work of the third angel."—EW 85, 86.

This third paragraph from the inspired pen indicates the conditions that are to exist in the earth as the work of salvation is at the point of reaching its conclusion. Notice that it states that trouble will be spreading over the earth, in accordance with the prophecy of Christ. Meanwhile the nations will be growing more and more angry.

And this is exactly what is happening in our days. The nations are angry. Disagreements among the most powerful countries of the world, and the selfish ambitions of some of them for universal domination, cause a yearly increase in military budgets, a strengthening of armies, and a substantial growth in the quantity and the offensive power of world armaments.

One war succeeds another. Peace-promoting agencies face crisis after crisis without effective means of preventing conflicts.

The fantastic store of destructive power in stockpiles of nuclear bombs and intercontinental ballistic missiles, and the tragic possibility that human society may be practically in ruins following a nuclear war, have created a state of despondent fear and desperate worry. Not only political leaders of the world, military men, and scientists, but all the people as well, sense that at any moment the whole earth may be involved in a truly cataclysmic holocaust.

Human hearts are full of trouble. Hunger scourges whole populations. Social disorders, strife, and racial uprisings constitute further proof that apprehension dominates humanity. Fear and despair have become the basic conditions of society. Agitation besets universities, factories, and the streets of great cities. There is disorientation among youth.

Delinquency is increasing to such an alarming extent that worried authorities cannot control it. It troubles parents, who may at any time be deprived of some family member by kidnapping; it troubles young women, who may be victims of immoral violence. It troubles men in general, whose security does not have any guarantee. Statistics constantly show a swelling wave of crime. One breathes the air of violence everywhere—it ambushes every step of modern man.

Other indisputable symptoms of increasing trouble are the growing number of suicides and the alarming figures on mental illness and psychic disorders. Two million people in the United States have attempted at least once to take their own lives, according to information from the American College of Neuropsychiatrists.

The disintegration of society—accompanied with vice, alcoholism, and drug addiction—complicates this panorama of disorientation, fear, and trouble. All these things proclaim the imminence of the hour in which the sun of divine mercy will set, the period of grace will end, and the short time of trouble will commence. They point us, as a people, to the glorious culmination of our dearest hopes.

But the nearness of the tremendous events which we expect before the liberation should induce us to seek a genuine experience with God. Only such preparation will protect us in the hour of peril.

CHAPTER 9

THE TIME OF TROUBLE

Synthesis—The close of probation—The four angels loose the winds—Description of the time of trouble—The time of Jacob's trouble—Physical and mental anguish—Why the trouble will be permitted—God's people pass through the time of trouble—Many will go to their rest before—No material provision will be of value—Divine refuge.

SYNTHESIS

THE TIME of trouble is a period of unknown duration, but certainly brief. It will begin with the decree of Revelation 22:11 —Heaven's pronouncement which ends the period of grace and probation (the opportunity of salvation)—and will last until the day of Christ's second coming.

Daniel 12:1 refers to the beginning of this time in these words: "And at that time shall Michael stand up." Michael is Christ. Jesus completes His intercessory work, puts off His priestly garments, goes out of the sanctuary, and puts on His royal robe.

By this time most Bible prophecies will have been fulfilled, the proclamation of the gospel will have been finished, the shaking and the sealing will have occurred, and the latter rain will have fallen.

During the time of trouble the seven plagues fall, bringing terrible punishment to the impenitent, but they do not fall on the children of God. The four angels of Revelation 7 have released the winds of strife, giving free rein to nature and men to cast off the restraint of law. The plagues descend unmixed with God's mercy, and without the restricting benevolent influence of the Holy Spirit, which will have been withdrawn from the earth.

The persecution, which will have commenced during the time of probation with the imposing of Sunday laws, will become more severe during the time of trouble, reaching maximum fierceness with the pronouncing of the death decree. But this decree will not be carried out, because at the expiration of the time God will liberate His people amidst a tremendous display of natural phenomena and fearful manifestations of His anger.

Under the sixth and seventh plagues Armageddon occurs, resulting in turmoil and bloodshed.

Although the faithful will not suffer the plagues and will be miraculously fed, guarded, and protected, they will nevertheless go through a terrible ordeal: (1) Physical hardship, because the persecution will force them to flee from all centers of population. (2) Mental anguish, because they feel deep concern about the forgiveness of all their sins. But finally peace and tranquillity take the place of anxiety because they cannot recall any unconfessed sin, all having been forsaken and forgiven during the period of grace.

Within the great time of trouble there is included a lesser time called "the time of Jacob's trouble." Jeremiah 30:7. It extends from the time of the death decree—and this after the plagues have already started to fall—to the liberation.

Only those who have received the refreshing and have been sealed are in a condition to pass safely through this stormy time, standing firmly to welcome with unspeakable joy the Lord Jesus at His second coming.

The time of trouble, during which there will be neither mediator nor pardon for sin, requires serious preparation of life and heart now.

THE CLOSE OF PROBATION

"Behold, I come as a thief. Blessed is he that watcheth, and keepeth his garments, lest he walk naked, and they see his shame." Revelation 16:15.

This passage applies to the way in which the end of the investigative judgment and the termination of the period of grace will come unsuspected. To this special moment the prophecy of Daniel 12:1 also refers: "And at that time shall Michael stand up, the great Prince which standeth for the children of thy people: and there shall be a time of trouble, such as never was since there was a nation even to that same time: and at that time thy people shall be delivered, everyone that shall be found written in the book."

From this instant on, the destiny of each person will remain forever fixed, because the following decree is then proclaimed: "He that is unjust, let him be unjust still: and he which is filthy, let him be filthy still: and he that is righteous, let him be righteous still: and he that is holy, let him be holy still. And, behold, I come quickly; and My reward is with Me, to give every man according as his work shall be." Revelation 22:11, 12.

Jesus, our great High Priest, who still intercedes for us in the heavenly sanctuary, will then have completed His mediatorial and priestly work.

"And the angel took the censer, and filled it with fire of the altar, and cast it into the earth: and there were voices, and thunderings, and lightnings, and an earthquake." Revelation 8:5.

"I saw Jesus, who had been ministering before the ark containing the Ten Commandments, throw down the censer. He raised His hands, and with a loud voice said, 'It is done.' "—EW 279.

"When the work of investigation shall be ended [the investigative judgment], when the cases of those who in all ages have professed to be followers of Christ have been examined and decided, then, and not till then, probation will close, and the door of mercy will be shut. Thus in the one short sentence, 'They that were ready went in with Him to the marriage: and the door was shut,' we are carried down through the Saviour's final ministration, to the time when the great work for man's salvation shall be completed."—GC 428.

"Silently, unnoticed as the midnight thief, will come the decisive hour which marks the fixing of every man's destiny, the final withdrawal of mercy's offer to guilty men."—GC 491.

"An angel returning from the earth announces that his work is done; the final test has been brought upon the world, and all who have proved themselves loyal to the divine precepts have received 'the seal of the living God.' Then Jesus ceases His intercession in the sanctuary above. He lifts His hands and with a loud voice says, 'It is done'; and all the angelic host lay off their crowns as He makes the solemn announcement: 'He that is unjust, let him be unjust still:

and he which is filthy, let him be filthy still: and he that is righteous, let him be righteous still: and he that is holy, let him be holy still.' Revelation 22:11. Every case has been decided for life or death."—GC 613.

"We are to bear the third angel's message to the world, warning men against the worship of the beast and his image, and directing them to take their places in the ranks of those who 'keep the commandments of God, and have the faith of Jesus.' God has not revealed to us the time when this message will close, or when probation will have an end. Those things that are revealed we shall accept for ourselves and for our children; but let us not seek to know that which has been kept secret in the councils of the Almighty. It is our duty to watch and work and wait, to labor every moment for the souls of men that are ready to perish."—RH, Oct. 9, 1894.

"Come when it may, the day of God will come unawares to the ungodly. When life is going on in its unvarying round; when men are absorbed in pleasure, in business, in traffic, in moneymaking; when religious leaders are magnifying the world's progress and enlightenment, and the people are lulled in a false security—then, as the midnight thief steals within the unguarded dwelling, so shall sudden destruction come upon the careless and ungodly, 'and they shall not escape.' "—GC 38.

"When God's presence was finally withdrawn from the Jewish nation, priests and people knew it not. Though under the control of Satan, and swayed by the most horrible and malignant passions, they still regarded themselves as the chosen of God. The ministration in the temple continued; sacrifices were offered upon its polluted altars, and daily the divine blessing was invoked upon a people guilty of the blood of God's dear Son and seeking to slay His ministers and apostles. So when the irrevocable decision of the sanctuary has been pronounced and the destiny of the world has been forever fixed, the inhabitants of the earth will know it not. The forms of religion will be continued by a people from whom the Spirit of God has been finally withdrawn; and the satanic zeal with which the prince of evil will inspire them for the accomplishment of his malignant designs, will bear the semblance of zeal for God."—GC 615.

"We are standing on the threshold of the crisis of the ages. . . . The angel of mercy cannot remain much longer to shelter the impenitent."—PK 278.

"The crisis is stealing gradually upon us. The sun shines in the heavens, passing over its usual round, and the heavens still declare the glory of God. Men are still eating and drinking, planting and building, marrying and giving in marriage. Merchants are still buying and selling. Men are jostling one against another, contending for the highest place. Pleasure lovers are still crowding to theaters, horse races, gambling hells. The highest excitement prevails, yet probation's hour is fast closing, and every case is about to be eternally decided. Satan sees that his time is short. He has set all his agencies at work that men may be deceived, deluded, occupied, and entranced until the day of probation shall be ended, and the door of mercy forever shut."—ChS 51.

"Transgression has almost reached its limit. Confusion fills the world, and a great terror is soon to come upon human beings. The end is very near."—8T 28.

THE FOUR ANGELS LOOSE THE WINDS

"I saw that the four angels would hold the four winds until Jesus' work was done in the sanctuary, and then will come the seven last plagues."—EW 36.

"John sees the elements of nature—earthquake, tempest, and political strife—represented as being held by four angels. These winds are under control until God gives the word to let them go. There is the safety of God's church. The angels of God do His bidding, holding back the winds of the earth, that the winds should not blow on the earth, nor on the sea, nor on any tree, until the servants of God should be sealed in their foreheads."—TM 444.

"It is the voice of this highest angel that had authority to command the four angels to keep in check the four winds until this work [the sealing] was performed, and until he should give the summons to let them loose."—TM 445.

"He will restrain the forces of darkness until the warning is given to the world and all who will heed it are prepared for the conflict."—5T 453 (2TT 153).

"But so long as Jesus remains man's intercessor in the sanctuary above, the restraining influence of the Holy Spirit is felt by rulers and people. It still controls to some extent the laws of the land. Were it not for these laws, the condition of the world would be much worse than it now is. While many of our rulers are active agents of Satan, God also has His agents among the leading men of the nation."—GC 610.

"While already nation is rising against nation, and kingdom against kingdom, there is not now a general engagement. As yet the four winds are held until the servants of God shall be sealed in their foreheads. Then the powers of earth will marshal their forces for the last great battle."—6T 14 (2TT 369).

"As Jesus moved out of the most holy place, I heard the tinkling of the bells upon His garment; and as He left, a cloud of darkness covered the inhabitants of the earth. There was then no mediator between guilty man and an offended God. While Jesus had been standing between God and guilty man, a restraint was upon the people; but when He stepped out from between man and the Father, the restraint was removed and Satan had entire control of the finally impenitent."—EW 280.

"The apostle John in vision heard a loud voice in heaven exclaiming: 'Woe to the inhabiters of the earth and of the sea! for the devil is come down unto you, having great wrath, because he knoweth that he hath but a short time.' Revelation 12:12. Fearful are the scenes which call forth this exclamation from the heavenly voice. The wrath of Satan increases as his time grows short, and his work of deceit and destruction will reach its culmination in the time of trouble."—GC 623.

DESCRIPTION OF THE TIME OF TROUBLE

"And at that time shall Michael stand up, the great Prince which standeth for the children of thy people: and there shall be a time of trouble, such as never was since there was a nation even to that same time: and at that time thy people shall be delivered, everyone that shall be found written in the book." Daniel 12:1.

"When He leaves the sanctuary, darkness* covers the inhabitants of the earth. In that fearful time the righteous must live in the sight of a holy God without an intercessor. The restraint which has been upon the wicked is removed, and Satan has entire control of the finally impenitent. God's long-suffering has ended. The world has rejected His mercy, despised His love, and trampled upon His law. The wicked have passed the boundary of their probation; the Spirit of God, persistently resisted, has been at last withdrawn. Unsheltered by divine grace, they have no protection from the wicked one. Satan will then plunge the inhabitants of the earth into one great, final trouble. As the angels of God cease to hold in check the fierce winds of human passion, all the elements of strife will be let loose. The whole world will be involved in ruin more terrible than that which came upon Jerusalem of old."—GC 614.

"The people of God will then be plunged into those scenes of affliction and distress described by the prophet as the time of Jacob's

*There is no evidence from the spirit of prophecy writings that this is a physical darkness or a physical sign of any kind.

trouble. 'Thus saith the Lord: We have heard a voice of trembling, of fear, and not of peace. . . . All faces are turned into paleness. Alas! for that day is great, so that none is like it: it is even the time of Jacob's trouble; but he shall be saved out of it.' Jeremiah 30:5-7." —GC 616.

"The time is at hand when there will be sorrow in the world that no human balm can heal."—PK 277.

"When Christ ceases His intercession in the sanctuary, the unmingled wrath threatened against those who worship the beast and his image and receive his mark (Revelation 14:9, 10), will be poured out."—GC 627.

"The 'time of trouble, such as never was,' is soon to open upon us; and we shall need an experience which we do not now possess and which many are too indolent to obtain."—GC 622.

"The world is stirred with the spirit of war. The prophecy of the eleventh chapter of Daniel has nearly reached its complete fulfillment. Soon the scenes of trouble spoken of in the prophecies will take place."—9T 14 (3TT 283).

"As the approach of the Roman armies was a sign to the disciples of the impending destruction of Jerusalem, so may this apostasy [Sunday legislation, the threefold alliance, and the repudiation of the principles of the American Constitution] be a sign to us that the limit of God's forbearance is reached, that the measure of our nation's iniquity is full, and that the angel of mercy is about to take her flight, never to return."—5T 451 (2TT 151).

THE TIME OF JACOB'S TROUBLE

"I saw that the four angels would hold the four winds until Jesus' work was done in the sanctuary, and then will come the seven last plagues. These plagues enraged the wicked against the righteous; they thought that we had brought the judgments of God upon them, and that *if they could rid the earth of us, the plagues would then be stayed. A decree went forth to slay the saints,* which caused them to cry day and night for deliverance. This was the time of Jacob's trouble. Then all the saints cried out with anguish of spirit, and were delivered by the voice of God."—EW 36, 37.

From this inspired paragraph we may draw two conclusions:

(1) The time of Jacob's trouble embraces the period which extends from the promulgation of the death decree to the liberation of the children of God, a time during which they call with anguish for divine intervention.

(2) The period begins after the plagues have started to fall. This we know because the death decree will be proclaimed after some of the plagues have already fallen. It is the suffering which the "plagues" bring (and note, the word appears in plural) that leads to the death decree.

PHYSICAL AND MENTAL ANGUISH

"Jacob's experience during that night of wrestling and anguish represents the trial through which the people of God must pass just before Christ's second coming."—PP 201.

(1) Jacob experienced anguish because of the *material situation* which confronted him: His brother was coming against him with 400 armed men, apparently with intentions of revenge. Also the saints will feel *anguish because of physical persecution and the death decree.*

(2) Furthermore, Jacob felt *intense mental anguish* in his struggle with God in prayer because he was not sure his sins had been pardoned. The saints will experience *similar anguish.* But even as Jacob's night ended with the blessing and the peace of God conferred on the patriarch, the Lord will fill His children with peace, confidence, and hope in the night of their greatest trial. And for the same reason—their sins, too, had previously all been confessed and forgiven.

The physical anguish: the persecution

"As the Sabbath has become the special point of controversy throughout Christendom, and religious and secular authorities have combined to enforce the observance of the Sunday, the persistent refusal of a small minority to yield to the popular demand will make them objects of universal execration. It will be urged that the few who stand in opposition to an institution of the church and a law of the state ought not to be tolerated; that it is better for them to suffer than for whole nations to be thrown into confusion and lawlessness. . . . This argument will appear conclusive; and a decree will finally be issued against those who hallow the Sabbath of the fourth commandment, denouncing them as deserving of the severest punishment and giving the people liberty, after a certain time, to put them to death. Romanism in the Old World and apostate Protestantism in the New will pursue a similar course toward those who honor all the divine precepts."—GC 615, 616.

"As the time appointed in the decree draws near, the people will conspire to root out the hated sect. It will be determined to strike in one night a decisive blow, which shall utterly silence the voice of dissent and reproof.

"The people of God—some in prison cells, some hidden in solitary retreats in the forests and the mountains—still plead for divine protection, while in every quarter companies of armed men, urged on by hosts of evil angels, are preparing for the work of death. It is now, in the hour of utmost extremity, that the God of Israel will interpose for the deliverance of His chosen."—GC 635.

"The Protestant world today see in the little company keeping the Sabbath a Mordecai in the gate. His character and conduct, expressing reverence for the law of God, are a constant rebuke to those who have cast off the fear of the Lord and are trampling upon His Sabbath; the unwelcome intruder must by some means be put out of the way."—5T 450 (2TT 150).

Mordecai—as related in the book of Esther—was a man of good intentions who gained royal favor by disclosing a plot against the king's life. Haman, great enemy of Mordecai and the Jewish people, had a gallows erected for executing Mordecai; but when he thought his plans were about to be realized, the exact opposite occurred. The gallows that had been prepared for Mordecai was used for the maker himself. The decree to kill the Jews was made of none effect and turned upon their enemies. The same will happen in the closing days of time. The enemies of truth will attempt to destroy those who keep the commandments of God; but God will intervene and liberate His people, and the enemies will be destroyed by their own weapons.

"As the decree issued by the various rulers of Christendom against the commandment keepers shall withdraw the protection of government and abandon them to those who desire their destruction, the people of God will flee from the cities and villages and associate together in companies, dwelling in the most desolate and solitary places. Many will find refuge in the strongholds of the mountains. Like the Christians of the Piedmont valleys, they will make the high places of the earth their sanctuaries and will thank God for 'the munitions of rocks.' Isaiah 33:16. But many of all nations and of all classes, high and low, rich and poor, black and white, will be cast into the most unjust and cruel bondage. The beloved of God pass weary days, bound in chains, shut in by prison bars, sentenced to be slain, some apparently left to die of starvation in dark and loathsome dungeons. No human ear is open to hear their moans; no human hand is ready to lend them help."—GC 626.

Under the subtitle "Divine Refuge" we shall see, a few pages farther along in this chapter, the beautiful counterpart of this situation, in God's protection and care for His children, in Christ's companionship with them, and in the ministration of angels in their behalf.

"Soon I saw the saints suffering great mental anguish. They seemed to be surrounded by the wicked inhabitants of the earth. Every appearance was against them. Some began to fear that God had at last left them to perish by the hand of the wicked. But if their eyes could have been opened, they would have seen themselves surrounded by angels of God."—EW 283.

"The people were at liberty after a certain time to put them to death. . . . Satan wished to have the privilege of destroying the saints of the Most High; but Jesus bade His angels watch over them. . . . Soon I saw the saints suffering great mental anguish. They seemed to be surrounded by the wicked inhabitants of the earth. . . . But the saints heeded them not. Like Jacob, they were wrestling with God."—EW 283, 284.

"The people of God will then be plunged into those scenes of affliction and distress which prophets have described as the time of Jacob's trouble. The cries of the faithful, persecuted ones ascend to heaven. And as the blood of Abel cried from the ground, there are voices also crying to God from martyrs' graves, from the sepulchers of the sea, from mountain caverns, from convent vaults: 'How long, O Lord, holy and true, dost Thou not judge and avenge our blood on them that dwell on the earth?' "—5T 451 (2TT 151).

"I saw measures taken against the company who had the light and power of God. Darkness thickened around them; yet they stood firm, approved of God, and trusting in Him. I saw them perplexed; next I heard them crying unto God earnestly. Day and night their cry ceased not: 'Thy will, O God, be done! If it can glorify Thy name, make a way of escape for Thy people! Deliver us from the heathen around about us. They have appointed us unto death; but Thine arm can bring salvation.' These are all the words which I can bring to mind. All seemed to have a deep sense of their unworthiness and manifested entire submission to the will of God; yet, like Jacob, everyone, without an exception, was earnestly pleading and wrestling for deliverance."—EW 272.

"It was an hour of fearful, terrible agony to the saints. Day and night they cried unto God for deliverance. To outward appearance, there was no possibility of their escape. The wicked had already begun to triumph, crying out, 'Why doesn't your God deliver you out of our hands? Why don't you go up and save your lives?' But the saints heeded them not."—EW 283.

The mental anguish

"Though God's people will be surrounded by enemies who are bent upon their destruction, yet the anguish which they suffer is not a dread of persecution for the truth's sake; they fear that every sin has not been repented of, and that through some fault in themselves they will fail to realize the fulfillment of the Saviour's promise. . . .

"Their faith does not fail because their prayers are not immediately answered. Though suffering the keenest anxiety, terror, and distress, they do not cease their intercessions. They lay hold of the strength of God as Jacob laid hold of the Angel; and the language of their souls is: 'I will not let Thee go, except Thou bless me.'"—GC 619, 620.

"As Satan accuses the people of God on account of their sins, the Lord permits him to try them to the uttermost. Their confidence in God, their faith and firmness, will be severely tested. As they review the past, their hopes sink; for in their whole lives they can see little good. They are fully conscious of their weakness and unworthiness. Satan endeavors to terrify them with the thought that their cases are hopeless, that the stain of their defilement will never be washed away. He hopes so to destroy their faith that they will yield to his temptations and turn from their allegiance to God."—GC 618, 619.

"Had not Jacob previously repented of his sin in obtaining the birthright by fraud, God would not have heard his prayer and mercifully preserved his life. So, in the time of trouble, if the people of God had unconfessed sins to appear before them while tortured with fear and anguish, they would be overwhelmed; despair would cut off their faith, and they could not have confidence to plead with God for deliverance. But while they have a deep sense of their unworthiness, they have no concealed wrongs to reveal. Their sins have gone beforehand to judgment and have been blotted out, and they cannot bring them to remembrance.

"Satan leads many to believe that God will overlook their unfaithfulness in the minor affairs of life; but the Lord shows in His dealings with Jacob that He will in no wise sanction or tolerate evil. All who endeavor to excuse or conceal their sins, and permit them to remain upon the books of heaven, unconfessed and unforgiven, will be overcome by Satan."—GC 620.

WHY THE TROUBLE WILL BE PERMITTED

"Those who exercise but little faith now, are in the greatest danger of falling under the power of satanic delusions and the decree to compel the conscience. And even if they endure the test they will be plunged into deeper distress and anguish in the time of trouble, because they have never made it a habit to trust in God. The lessons of faith which they have neglected they will be forced to learn under a terrible pressure of discouragement."—GC 622.

"The assaults of Satan are fierce and determined, his delusions are terrible; but the Lord's eye is upon His people; and His ear listens to their cries. Their affliction is great, the flames of the furnace seem about to consume them; but the Refiner will bring them forth as gold tried in the fire. God's love for His children during the period of their severest trial is as strong and tender as in the days of their sunniest prosperity; but it is needful for them to be placed in the furnace of fire; their earthliness must be consumed, that the image of Christ may be perfectly reflected."—GC 621.

"The people of God must drink of the cup and be baptized with the baptism. The very delay, so painful to them, is the best answer to their petitions. As they endeavor to wait trustingly for the Lord to work they are led to exercise faith, hope, and patience, which have been too little exercised during their religious experience."—GC 630, 631.

GOD'S PEOPLE PASS THROUGH THE TIME OF TROUBLE

"None but the hundred and forty-four thousand can learn that song; for it is the song of their experience—an experience such as no other company have ever had. . . . These, having been translated from the earth, from among the living, are counted as 'the firstfruits unto God and to the Lamb.' . . . They have passed through the time of trouble such as never was since there was a nation; they have endured the anguish of the time of Jacob's trouble."—GC 649.

MANY WILL GO TO THEIR REST BEFORE

"Many will be laid away to sleep before the fiery ordeal of the time of trouble shall come upon our world. This is another reason why we should say after our earnest petition: 'Nevertheless not my will, but Thine, be done.' Luke 22:42."—CH 375.

NO MATERIAL PROVISION WILL BE OF VALUE

"The Lord has shown me repeatedly that it is contrary to the Bible to make any provision for our temporal wants in the time of trouble. I saw that if the saints had food laid up by them or in the field in the time of trouble, when sword, famine, and pestilence are in the land, it would be taken from them by violent hands and strangers would reap their fields."—EW 56.

"I was shown that it is the will of God that the saints should cut loose from every encumbrance before the time of trouble comes, and make a covenant with God through sacrifice. If they have their property on the altar and earnestly inquire of God for duty, He will teach them when to dispose of these things. Then they will be free in the time of trouble and have no clogs to weigh them down."—EW 56, 57.

"I also saw that God had not required all of His people to dispose of their property at the same time; but if they desired to be taught, He would teach them, in a time of need, when to sell and how much to sell."—EW 57.

DIVINE REFUGE

"He shall dwell on high: his place of defense shall be the munitions of rocks: bread shall be given him; his waters shall be sure." Isaiah 33:16.

"Surely He shall deliver thee from the snare of the fowler, and from the noisome pestilence. He shall cover thee with His feathers, and under His wings shalt thou trust: His truth shall be thy shield and buckler. Thou shalt not be afraid for the terror by night; nor for the arrow that flieth by day; nor for the pestilence that walketh in darkness; nor for the destruction that wasteth at noonday. A thousand shall fall at thy side, and ten thousand at thy right hand; but it shall not come nigh thee. Only with thine eyes shalt thou behold and see the reward of the wicked. Because thou hast made the Lord, which is my refuge, even the Most High, thy habitation; there shall no evil befall thee, neither shall any plague come nigh thy dwelling." Psalm 91:3-10.

"God is our refuge and strength, a very present help in trouble. Therefore will not we fear, though the earth be removed, and though the mountains be carried into the midst of the sea;

though the waters thereof roar and be troubled, though the mountains shake with the swelling thereof." "The heathen raged, the kingdoms were moved: He uttered His voice, the earth melted. The Lord of hosts is with us; the God of Jacob is our refuge. Come, behold the works of the Lord, what desolations he hath made in the earth. He maketh wars to cease unto the end of the earth; he breaketh the bow, and cutteth the spear in sunder; he burneth the chariot in the fire." Psalm 46:1-3, 6-9.

"But to the obedient is given the promise, 'He shall dwell on high: his place of defense shall be the munitions of rocks: bread shall be given him; his waters shall be sure.' Isaiah 33:16. By this promise the children of God will live. When the earth shall be wasted with famine, they shall be fed. 'They shall not be ashamed in the evil time: and in the days of famine they shall be satisfied.' Psalm 37:19. To that time of distress the prophet Habakkuk looked forward, and his words express the faith of the church: 'Although the fig tree shall not blossom, neither shall fruit be in the vines; the labor of the olive shall fail, and the fields shall yield no meat; the flock shall be cut off from the fold, and there shall be no herd in the stalls: yet I will rejoice in the Lord, I will joy in the God of my salvation.' Habakkuk 3:17, 18."—DA 122.

"The people of God will not be free from suffering; but while persecuted and distressed, while they endure privation and suffer for want of food they will not be left to perish. That God who cared for Elijah will not pass by one of His self-sacrificing children. He who numbers the hairs of their head will care for them, and in time of famine they shall be satisfied."—GC 629.

"I saw the saints leaving the cities and villages, and associating together in companies, and living in the most solitary places. Angels provided them food and water, while the wicked were suffering from hunger and thirst. Then I saw the leading men of the earth consulting together, and Satan and his angels busy around them. I saw a writing, copies of which were scattered in different parts of the land, giving orders that unless the saints should yield their peculiar faith, give up the Sabbath, and observe the first day of the week, the people were at liberty after a certain time to put them to death. But in this hour of trial the saints were calm and composed, trusting in God and leaning upon His promise that a way of escape would be made for them. In some places, before the time for the decree to be executed, the wicked rushed upon the saints to slay them; but angels in the form of men of war fought for them."—EW 282, 283.

"They [God's children] seemed to be surrounded by the wicked inhabitants of the earth. Every appearance was against them. . . . But if their eyes could have been opened, they would have seen themselves surrounded by angels of God. Next came the multitude of the angry wicked, and next a mass of evil angels, hurrying on the wicked to slay the saints. But before they could approach God's people, the wicked must first pass this company of mighty, holy angels. This was impossible. The angels of God were causing them to recede and also causing the evil angels who were pressing around them to fall back.

"It was an hour of fearful, terrible agony to the saints. Day and night they cried unto God for deliverance. To outward appearance, there was no possibility of their escape. The wicked had already begun to triumph, crying out, 'Why doesn't your God deliver you out of our hands? Why don't you go up and save your lives?' But the saints heeded them not. . . . The angels longed to deliver them, but they must wait a little longer. . . . The time had nearly come when He was to manifest His mighty power and gloriously deliver His saints."—EW 283, 284.

"I saw that God will in a wonderful manner preserve His people through the time of trouble. As Jesus poured out His soul in agony in the garden, they will earnestly cry and agonize day and night for deliverance. The decree will go forth that they must disregard the Sabbath of the fourth commandment, and honor the first day, or lose their lives; but they will not yield, and trample under their feet the Sabbath of the Lord, and honor an institution of papacy. Satan's host and wicked men will surround them, and exult over them, because there will seem to be no way of escape for them. But in the midst of their revelry and triumph, there is heard peal upon peal of the loudest thunder. The heavens have gathered blackness, and are only illuminated by the blazing light and terrible glory from heaven, as God utters His voice from His holy habitation."—1T 353, 354 (1TT 131).

"In the midst of the time of trouble—trouble such as has not been since there was a nation—His chosen ones will stand unmoved. Satan with all the hosts of evil cannot destroy the weakest of God's saints. Angels that excel in strength will protect them, and in their behalf Jehovah will reveal Himself as a 'God of gods,' able to save to the uttermost those who have put their trust in Him."—PK 513.

"While the wicked are dying from hunger and pestilence, angels will shield the righteous and supply their wants. To him that 'walketh righteously' is the promise: 'Bread shall be given him; his waters shall be sure.' 'When the poor and needy seek water, and there is none, and their tongue faileth for thirst, I the Lord will hear them, I the God of Israel will not forsake them.' Isaiah 33:15, 16; 41:17."— GC 629.

"The darkest hour of the church's struggle with the powers of evil is that which immediately precedes the day of her final deliverance. But none who trust in God need fear; for 'when the blast of the terrible ones is as a storm against the wall,' God will be to His church 'a refuge from the storm.' Isaiah 25:4."—PK 725.

"In the time of trouble just before the coming of Christ, the righteous will be preserved through the ministration of heavenly angels; but there will be no security for the transgressor of God's law. Angels cannot then protect those who are disregarding one of the divine precepts."—PP 256.

"I saw a covering that God was drawing over His people to protect them in the time of trouble; and every soul that was decided on the truth and was pure in heart was to be covered with the covering of the Almighty."—EW 43.

"The world see the very class whom they have mocked and derided, and desired to exterminate, pass unharmed through pestilence, tempest, and earthquake. He who is to the transgressors of His law a devouring fire, is to His people a safe pavilion."—GC 654.

"Like the captive exile, they will be in fear of death by starvation or by violence. But the Holy One who divided the Red Sea before Israel, will manifest His mighty power and turn their captivity."— GC 634.

"Fearful tests and trials await the people of God. The spirit of war is stirring the nations from one end of the earth to the other. But in the midst of the time of trouble that is coming,—a time of trouble such as has not been since there was a nation,—God's chosen people will stand unmoved. Satan and his host cannot destroy them, for angels that excel in strength will protect them."—9T 17 (3TT 285).

CHAPTER 10

THE PLAGUES

Synthesis—General considerations on the plagues: description, time, extent, duration, protection of the sealed, hunger for the Word of God—The sixth and seventh plagues: Armageddon—Despair of the wicked.

SYNTHESIS

THE POURING OUT of the seven last plagues covers the same period as the time of trouble. Once probation ends and the temple is filled with smoke, our great High Priest, Christ Jesus, leaves the temple and ceases His intercessory work. Upon the wicked inhabitants of the earth the most terrible judgments of God will then be poured out.

While the righteous, who have received the seal of the living God, are marvelously protected from all physical harm, the wicked suffer the scourges of divine wrath. Because God withdraws His protection from the earth (save for His children), the great enemy is left with a free hand to demonstrate the nature of his government, and the rejecters of divine grace are punished without mercy.

A description of the plagues can be read in the sixteenth chapter of Revelation. Here is a summary of their nature:

First: A noisome and grievous sore upon those who have the mark of the beast.

Second: The sea becomes as blood, and every living soul in the sea dies.

Third: The rivers and fountains of water become blood, because the wicked have shed the blood of the saints.

Fourth: The sun scorches man with fire.

Fifth: This plague is poured out on the throne of the beast (Rome), and his kingdom is full of darkness. The wicked gnaw their tongues for pain.

Sixth: The sixth plague is poured out upon the Euphrates; its water is dried up, and the battle of Armageddon begins.

Seventh: This plague is poured out into the air, and a series of spectacular events takes place, which paralyze the wicked and cause the final deliverance of the children of God. Then comes the majestic appearance of Christ, with its accompanying events.

It is not the purpose of this chapter to make a complete and analytic study of all the plagues, but rather to consider some aspects of the sixth and the seventh ones, the two which relate to the main subject of this book.

GENERAL CONSIDERATIONS ON THE PLAGUES

Description

Read Revelation 16.

"A noise shall come even to the ends of the earth; for the Lord hath a controversy with the nations, He will plead with all flesh; He will give them that are wicked to the sword, saith the Lord." Jeremiah 25:31.

"The apostle John in vision heard a loud voice in heaven exclaiming: 'Woe to the inhabiters of the earth and of the sea! for the devil is come down unto you, having great wrath, because he knoweth that he hath but a short time.' Revelation 12:12. Fearful are the scenes which call forth this exclamation from the heavenly voice. The wrath of Satan increases as his time grows short, and his work of deceit and destruction will reach its culmination in the time of trouble."—GC 623.

"The plagues upon Egypt when God was about to deliver Israel were similar in character to those more terrible and extensive judgments which are to fall upon the world just before the final deliverance of God's people. Says the revelator, in describing those terrific scourges: 'There fell a noisome and grievous sore upon the men which had the mark of the beast, and upon them which worshiped his image.' The sea 'became as the blood of a dead man: and every living soul died in the sea.' And 'the rivers and fountains of waters . . . became blood.' Terrible as these inflictions are, God's justice stands fully vindicated. The angel of God declares: 'Thou art righteous, O Lord, . . . because Thou hast judged thus. For they have shed the blood of saints and prophets, and Thou hast given them blood to drink; for they are worthy.' Revelation 16:2-6."—GC 627, 628.

Time

The falling of the plagues takes place during the time when the temple is closed and filled with smoke. Revelation 15:8. In other words, they come after the end of probation and during the time of trouble.

"It was impossible for the plagues to be poured out while Jesus officiated in the sanctuary; but as His work there is finished, and His intercession closes, there is nothing to stay the wrath of God, and it breaks with fury upon the shelterless head of the guilty sinner, who has slighted salvation and hated reproof."—EW 280.

Extent

"These plagues are not universal, or the inhabitants of the earth would be wholly cut off. Yet they will be the most awful scourges that have ever been known to mortals. All the judgments upon men, prior to the close of probation, have been mingled with mercy. The pleading blood of Christ has shielded the sinner from receiving the full measure of his guilt; but in the final judgment, wrath is poured out unmixed with mercy."—GC 628, 629.

Duration

The duration will be brief. If the word "day" mentioned in Revelation 18:8 is prophetic time ("Her plagues come in one day"), and if we apply the prophetic scale of "each day for a year" (Ezekiel 4:6), it may be reasoned that the plagues will last for a year. The spirit of prophecy makes no reference to the length of the period. *The S.D.A. Bible Commentary* suggests that the original language would "stress suddenness and unexpectedness rather than duration."

Protection of the sealed

The children of God will be miraculously protected from the plagues. Psalm 91.

"While the wicked are dying from hunger and pestilence, angels will shield the righteous and supply their wants. To him that 'walketh righteously' is the promise: 'Bread shall be given him; his waters shall be sure.' 'When the poor and needy seek water, and there is none, and their tongue faileth for thirst, I the Lord will hear them, I the God of Israel will not forsake them.' Isaiah 33:15, 16; 41:17."—GC 629.

Hunger for the Word of God

"In that day, multitudes will desire the shelter of God's mercy which they have so long despised. "Behold, the days come, saith the Lord God, that I will send a famine in the land, not a famine of bread, nor a thirst for water, but of hearing the words of the Lord: and they shall wander from sea to sea, and from the north even to the east, they shall run to and fro to seek the word of the Lord, and shall not find it.' Amos 8:11, 12."—GC 629.

"Others rushed to the people of God and begged to be taught how they might escape His judgments. But the saints had nothing for them. The last tear for sinners had been shed, the last agonizing prayer offered, the last burden borne, the last warning given."—EW 281.

THE SIXTH AND SEVENTH PLAGUES: ARMAGEDDON

Armageddon starts under the sixth plague and ends under the seventh. Still an unfulfilled prophecy, some of its elements—especially the interpretation of its political aspects—are uncertain. It is not surprising, therefore, that several hypotheses regarding them have been advanced.

It is not the purpose of this book to go into these aspects or to make pronouncements about the drying up of the Euphrates, the preparation of the way of the kings of the East, and the political aspects of the great conflict.

We are vitally interested, nevertheless, in the essential features of the prophecy. Concerning these, no differences exist, because its certain interpretation is based on the Word of God, amply confirmed by the spirit of prophecy.

The word "Armageddon" is used just once in all the Scriptures. (Revelation 16:16.) It probably does not correspond to a definitely known geographical place. It could be taken as a symbolic expression, used by the Scriptures to refer not to a definite point in the world, but to a worldwide battle in the great day of God. This is a matter not altogether clear.

Says the apostle: "And I saw three unclean spirits like frogs come out of the mouth of the dragon, and out of the mouth of the beast, and out of the mouth of the false prophet. For they are the spirits of devils, working miracles, which go forth unto the kings of the earth and of the whole world, to gather them to the battle of that great day of God Almighty." Revelation 16: 13, 14.

Comparative analysis of this text with other Scripture passages and pertinent paragraphs from the spirit of prophecy lead to the following conclusions about Armageddon:

1. It is a battle between truth and error.
2. It is a conflict between Christ and Satan.
3. The fallen angels will take part in it.
4. The struggle will be directed against the children of God and will bring about a great persecution.
5. The apostate powers (the dragon, or spiritualism; the beast, or Romanism; and the false prophet, or apostate Protestantism) will participate actively in it. See also Revelation 19:20, 21.
6. The kings of the earth will be engaged in the battle, and their participation will cause a conflict of a political-military character.

In other words, Armageddon is the final act in the agelong drama of strife between good and evil, between Christ and Satan with their respective followings of angels and men, between truth and error.

In this battle three great powers will ally themselves under the prince of darkness: the dragon (spiritualism), the beast (the papacy), and the false prophet (apostate Protestantism). They will unite in the common purpose of fighting against God, leveling their attack at Him through the person of His faithful children. They will require all to receive the mark of the beast (Revelation 13:16) and will persecute the faithful, relying on the aid of kings to enforce its decrees. Those who refuse to comply will finally be sentenced to death.

Behind the scenes, directing in all this activity, will be "unclean spirits," who "are the spirits of devils." They will persuade the different governments to form an alliance and take part in this tremendous "battle of the great day of God Almighty." The assault will reach its climax immediately before Christ shall come the second time. See the next verse, Revelation 16:15:

"Behold, I come as a thief. Blessed is he that watcheth, and keepeth his [spiritual] garments."

The contending forces in the conflict will be formed, therefore, of the following: (1) Those arrayed against God—Satan, the demons, the political-religious persecuting powers, the kings of earth, and wicked men. (2) Those allied with God—Christ and His angels, and the righteous of earth who uphold truth and profess loyalty to the Creator and His law.

Chapter 19:11-21 refers, it would seem, to the same great battle, in which the Rider of the white horse, the King of kings and Lord of lords, contends with the wicked nations and subdues them and slays them with the sword which proceeds out of His mouth. Verse 21. The beast and the false prophet were cast into the lake of fire (verse 20), where finally also will be thrown the dragon in person, Satan, with all his angels. Revelation 20:10. This describes the final triumph of Christ, the truth, and the people of God.

Wrote the servant of the Lord:

"We need to study the pouring out of the seventh vial. The powers of evil will not yield up the conflict without a struggle. But Providence has a part to act in the battle of Armageddon. When the earth is lighted with the glory of the angel of Revelation eighteen, the religious elements, good and evil, will awake from slumber, and the armies of the living God will take the field."—7BC 983.

"A terrible conflict is before us. We are nearing the battle of the great day of God Almighty. That which has been held in control is to be let loose. The angel of mercy is folding her wings, preparing to step down from the throne, and leave the world to the control of Satan. The principalities and powers of earth are in bitter revolt against the God of heaven. They are filled with hatred against those who serve Him, and soon, very soon, will be fought the last great battle between good and evil. The earth is to be the battlefield—the scene of the final contest and the final victory. Here, where for so long Satan has led men against God, rebellion is to be forever suppressed."—RH, May 13, 1902.

"The last great conflict between truth and error is but the final struggle of the long-standing controversy concerning the law of God."—GC 582.

The ecumenical movement will progress not only in the United States but also in Rome. Protestantism and Catholicism unite, and when the papacy and spiritualism, together with apostate Protestantism, form an alliance, then only the small group obedient to God's commandments will be stigmatized as different and false for not uniting with the rest.

"All who have not the spirit of truth will unite under the leadership of satanic agencies. But *they are to be kept under control till the time shall come for the great battle of Armageddon.*"—7BC 967.

"Satan has long been preparing for his final effort to deceive the world. The foundation of his work was laid by the assurance given to Eve in Eden: 'Ye shall not surely die.' 'In the day ye eat therefore, then your eyes shall be opened, and ye shall be as gods, knowing good and evil.' Genesis 3:4, 5. Little by little he has prepared the way for his masterpiece of deception in the development of spiritualism. He has not yet reached the full accomplishment of his designs; but it will be reached in the last remnant of time. Says the prophet: 'I saw three unclean spirits like frogs; . . . they are the spirits of devils, working miracles, which go forth unto the kings of the earth and of the whole world, to gather them to the battle of that great day of God Almighty.' Revelation 16:13, 14."—GC 561, 562.

"Fearful sights of a supernatural character will soon be revealed in the heavens, in token of the power of miracle-working demons. *The spirits of devils will go forth to the kings of the earth and to the whole world, to fasten them in deception, and urge them on to unite with Satan in his last struggle against the government of heaven.* By these agencies, rulers and subjects will be alike deceived. Persons will arise pretending to be Christ Himself, and claiming the title and worship which belong to the world's Redeemer. *They will perform wonderful miracles of healing* and will profess to have revelations from heaven contradicting the testimony of the Scriptures."—GC 624.

But the final result of the battle of Armageddon will be the decisive triumph of Christ and His church, of God and His truth. Declares the seer of Patmos: "These shall make war with the Lamb, and the Lamb shall overcome them: for He is Lord of lords, and Kings of kings: and they that are with Him are called, and chosen, and faithful." Revelation 17:14.

Moreover, in the final verses of Revelation 19 is presented the capture of the beast and the false prophet, who are cast out into the lake of fire and brimstone, and the death of the other warriors, enemies of the Lord, who are killed by the sword that comes out of the mouth of the Rider, Jesus Himself.

DESPAIR OF THE WICKED

"When the voice of God turns the captivity of His people, there is a terrible awakening of those who have lost all in the great conflict of life. . . . Now they are stripped of all that made them great and are left destitute and defenseless. They look with terror upon the destruction of the idols which they preferred before their Maker. They have sold their souls for earthly riches and enjoyments, and have not sought to become rich toward God. The result is, their lives are a failure; their pleasures are now turned to gall, their treasures to corruption. The gain of a lifetime is swept away in a moment."—GC 654.

"The Lord cometh out of His place to punish the inhabitants of the earth for their iniquity: the earth also shall disclose her blood, and shall no more cover her slain." Isaiah 26:21. "And this shall be the plague wherewith the Lord will smite all the people that have fought against Jerusalem." Zechariah 14:12.

"Many of the wicked were greatly enraged as they suffered the effects of the plagues. It was a scene of fearful agony. Parents were bitterly reproaching their children, and children their parents, brothers their sisters, and sisters their brothers. Loud, wailing cries were heard in every direction, 'It was you who kept me from receiving the truth which would have saved me from this awful hour.' The people turned upon their ministers with bitter hate and reproached them, saying, 'You have not warned us. You told us that all the world was to be converted, and cried, Peace, peace, to quiet every fear that was aroused. You have not told us of this hour; and those who warned us of it you declared to be fanatics and evil men, who would ruin us.' But I saw that the ministers did not escape the wrath of God. Their suffering was tenfold greater than that of their people."—EW 282.

"The people see that they have been deluded. They accuse one another of having led them to destruction; but all unite in heaping their bitterest condemnation upon the ministers. Unfaithful pastors have prophesied smooth things; they have led their hearers to make void the law of God and to persecute those who would keep it holy. Now, in their despair, these teachers confess before the world their work of deception. The multitudes are filled with fury. 'We are lost!' they cry, 'and you are the cause of our ruin'; and they turn upon the false shepherds. The very ones that once admired them most will pronounce the most dreadful curses upon them. The very hands that once crowned them with laurels will be raised for their destruction. The swords which were to slay God's people are now employed to destroy their enemies. Everywhere there is strife and bloodshed."—GC 655, 656.

CHAPTER 11

THE END OF THE SEVENTH PLAGUE: DELIVERANCE

Important events—An account of the liberation—At midnight—Mighty manifestations of God's power—A crown of immortal glory—A sudden change in the scene—Cataclysmic events—A wonderful star of hope—The glorious cloud that surrounds the Prince of Life.

WHEN THE SEVENTH ANGEL pours out his vial, the most dreadful and strange manifestations of the elements take place, and the Lord puts an end to Armageddon with the most formidable demonstration of His power. Babylon comes into remembrance and receives her final reward. Also "the cities of the nations" fall, and all who participated in the persecution are punished.

IMPORTANT EVENTS

Following are listed the most important events under the seventh plague, at the conclusion of Armageddon, and a little before the second coming of Christ:

1. A great voice from heaven proclaims: "It is done."
2. Lightnings, voices, and thunders.
3. A gigantic earthquake, greatest in history.
4. The great city, spiritual Babylon (Rome), is divided into three parts; it comes in remembrance from God.
5. The other "cities of the nations" fall.
6. Islands flee and mountains disappear.
7. Hail falls from heaven, each hailstone the weight of a talent.

AN ACCOUNT OF LIBERATION

Then comes the liberation of the saints, described as follows:

"The Lord is doing His work. All heaven is astir. The Judge of all the earth is soon to arise and vindicate His insulted authority. The mark of deliverance will be set upon the men who keep God's commandments, who revere His law, and who refuse the mark of the beast or of his image."—5T 451, 452 (2TT 151).

"When the defiance of the law of Jehovah shall be almost universal, when His people shall be pressed in affliction by their fellow men, God will interpose. The fervent prayers of His people will be answered."—RH, June 15, 1897.

"The people of God—some in prison cells, some hidden in solitary retreats in the forests and the mountains—still plead for divine protection, while in every quarter companies of armed men, urged on by hosts of evil angels, are preparing for the work of death. It is now, in the hour of utmost extremity, that the God of Israel will interpose for the deliverance of His chosen."—GC 635.

"Then all the saints cried out with anguish of spirit, and were delivered by the voice of God. The 144,000 triumphed. Their faces were lighted up with the glory of God."—EW 37.

AT MIDNIGHT

"It was at midnight that God chose to deliver His people. As the wicked were mocking around them, suddenly the sun appeared, shining in his strength, and the moon stood still. The wicked looked upon the scene with amazement, while the saints beheld with solemn joy the tokens of their deliverance."—EW 285.

"In a moment shall they die, and the people shall be troubled at midnight, and pass away: and the mighty shall be taken away without hand." Job 34:20.

MIGHTY MANIFESTATIONS OF GOD'S POWER

"In the time of trouble* we all fled from the cities and villages, but were pursued by the wicked, who entered the houses of the saints

---

*In this passage the Lord's messenger, carried ahead in vision and viewing the events as they shall transpire, narrates in the first person plural what she saw in vision. This does not necessarily mean that she will participate in person in the future events described by her. The case is similar to that of Paul, who includes himself among those who will be alive and (not among the resurrected righteous) when Christ comes: "The dead in Christ shall rise first: then we which are alive and remain shall be caught up together with them." 1 Thessalonians 4: 15-17; see also 1 Corinthians 15:51, 52.

with a sword. They raised the sword to kill us, but it broke, and fell as powerless as a straw. Then we all cried day and night for deliverance, and the cry came up before God. The sun came up, and the moon stood still. The streams ceased to flow. Dark, heavy clouds came up and clashed against each other. But there was one clear place of settled glory, whence came the voice of God like many waters, which shook the heavens and the earth. The sky opened and shut and was in commotion. The mountains shook like a reed in the wind, and cast out ragged rocks all around. The sea boiled like a pot and cast out stones upon the land. And as God spoke the day and the hour of Jesus' coming and delivered the everlasting covenant to His people, He spoke one sentence, and then paused, while the words were rolling through the earth. The Israel of God stood with their eyes fixed upward, listening to the words as they came from the mouth of Jehovah, and rolled through the earth like peals of loudest thunder. It was awfully solemn. And at the end of every sentence the saints shouted, 'Glory! Alleluia!' Their countenances were lighted up with the glory of God; and they shone with the glory, as did the face of Moses when he came down from Sinai. The wicked could not look on them for the glory. And when the never-ending blessing was pronounced on those who had honored God in keeping His Sabbath holy, there was a mighty shout of victory over the beast and over his image."—EW 34.

"Satan's host and wicked men will surround them, and exult over them, because there will seem to be no way of escape for them. But in the midst of their revelry and triumph, there is heard peal upon peal of the loudest thunder. The heavens have gathered blackness, and are only illuminated by the blazing light and terrible glory from heaven, as God utters His voice from His holy habitation.

"The foundations of the earth shake; buildings totter and fall with a terrible crash. The sea boils like a pot, and the whole earth is in terrible commotion. The captivity of the righteous is turned, and with sweet and solemn whisperings they say to one another: 'We are delivered. It is the voice of God.'"—1T 354 (1TT 132).

A CROWN OF IMMORTAL GLORY

"Christ, the almighty Victor, holds out to His weary soldiers a crown of immortal glory; and His voice comes from the gates ajar: 'Lo, I am with you. Be not afraid. I am acquainted with all your sorrows; I have borne your griefs. You are not warring against untried enemies. I have fought the battle in your behalf, and in My name you are more than conquerors.'"—GC 633.

"And the heaven departed as a scroll when it is rolled together; and every mountain and island were moved out of their places." Revelation 6:14.

"Then the sun, moon, and stars will be moved out of their places. They will not pass away, but be shaken by the voice of God."—EW 41.

"Signs and wonders followed in quick succession. Everything seemed turned out of its natural course. The streams ceased to flow. Dark, heavy clouds came up and clashed against each other."—EW 285.

"Christ has spoken: Come, My people, enter thou into thy chambers, and shut thy doors about thee: hide thyself as it were for a little moment, until the indignation be overpast. For, behold, the Lord cometh out of His place to punish the inhabitants of the earth for their iniquity.' Isaiah 26:20, 21. Glorious will be the deliverance of those who have patiently waited for His coming and whose names are written in the book of life."—GC 634.

A SUDDEN CHANGE IN THE SCENE

The last events are described more fully in *The Great Controversy:*

"With shouts of triumph, jeering, and imprecation, throngs of evil men are about to rush upon their prey, when, lo, a dense blackness, deeper than the darkness of the night, falls upon the earth. Then a rainbow, shining with the glory from the throne of God, spans the heavens and seems to encircle each praying company. The angry multitudes are suddenly arrested. Their mocking cries die away. The objects of their murderous rage are forgotten. With fearful forebodings they gaze upon the symbol of God's covenant and long to be shielded from its overpowering brightness.

"By the people of God a voice, clear and melodious, is heard, saying, 'Look up,' and lifting their eyes to the heavens, they behold the bow of promise. The black, angry clouds that covered the firmament are parted, and like Stephen they look up steadfastly into heaven and see the glory of God and the Son of man seated upon His throne. In His divine form they discern the marks of His humiliation; and from His lips they hear the request presented before His Father and the holy angels: 'I will that they also, whom Thou hast given Me, be with Me where I am.' John 17:24. Again a voice, musical and triumphant, is heard, saying: 'They come! they come! holy, harmless, and undefiled. They have kept the word of My patience; they shall walk among the angels'; and the pale, quivering lips of those who have held fast their faith utter a shout of victory.

"It is at midnight that God manifests His power for the deliverance of His people. The sun appears, shining in its strength. Signs and wonders follow in quick succession. The wicked look with terror and amazement upon the scene, while the righteous behold with solemn joy the tokens of their deliverance. Everything in nature seems turned out of its course. The streams cease to flow. Dark, heavy clouds come up and clash against each other. In the midst of the angry heavens is one clear space of indescribable glory, whence comes the voice of God like the sound of many waters, saying: 'It is done.' Revelation 16:17.

CATACLYSMIC EVENTS

"That voice shakes the heavens and the earth. There is a mighty earthquake, 'such as was not since men were upon the earth, so mighty an earthquake, and so great.' Verses 17, 18. The firmament appears to open and shut. The glory from the throne of God seems flashing through. The mountains shake like a reed in the wind, and ragged rocks are scattered on every side. There is a roar as of a coming tempest. The sea is lashed into fury. There is heard the shriek of a hurricane like the voice of demons upon a mission of destruction. The whole earth heaves and swells like the waves of the sea. Its surface is breaking up. Its very foundations seem to be giving way. Mountain chains are sinking. Inhabited islands disappear. The seaports that have become like Sodom for wickedness are swallowed up by the angry waters. Babylon the great has come in remembrance before God, 'to give unto her the cup of the wine of the fierceness of His wrath.' Great hailstones, every one 'about the weight of a talent,' are doing their work of destruction. Verses 19, 21. The proudest cities of the earth are laid low. The lordly palaces, upon which the world's great men have lavished their wealth in order to glorify themselves, are crumbling to ruin before their eyes. Prison walls are rent asunder, and God's people, who have been held in bondage for their faith, are set free.

"Graves are opened, and 'many of them that sleep in the dust of the earth . . . awake, some to everlasting life, and some to shame and everlasting contempt.' Daniel 12:2. All who have died in the faith of the third angel's message come forth from the tomb glorified, to hear God's covenant of peace with those who have kept His law. 'They also which pierced Him' (Revelation 1:7), those that mocked and derided Christ's dying agonies, and the most violent opposers of His truth and His people, are raised to behold Him in His glory and to see the honor placed upon the loyal and obedient.

"Thick clouds still cover the sky; yet the sun now and then breaks through, appearing like the avenging eye of Jehovah. Fierce lightnings leap from the heavens, enveloping the earth in a sheet of flame. Above the terrific roar of thunder, voices, mysterious and awful, declare the doom of the wicked. The words spoken are not comprehended by all; but they are distinctly understood by the false teachers. Those who a little before were so reckless, so boastful and defiant, so exultant in their cruelty to God's commandment-keeping people, are now overwhelmed with consternation and shuddering in fear. Their wails are heard above the sound of the elements. Demons acknowledge the deity of Christ and tremble before His power, while men are supplicating for mercy and groveling in abject terror."—GC 635-638.

A WONDERFUL STAR OF HOPE

"Through a rift in the clouds there beams a star whose brilliancy is increased fourfold in contrast with the darkness. It speaks hope and joy to the faithful, but severity and wrath to the transgressors of God's law. Those who have sacrificed all for Christ are now secure, hidden as in the secret of the Lord's pavilion. They have been tested, and before the world and the despisers of truth they have evinced their fidelity to Him who died for them. A marvelous change has come over those who have held fast their integrity in the very face of death. They have been suddenly delivered from the dark and terrible tyranny of men transformed to demons. Their faces, so lately pale, anxious, and haggard, are now aglow with wonder, faith, and love. Their voices rise in triumphant song: 'God is our refuge and strength, a very present help in trouble. Therefore will not we fear, though the earth be removed, and though the mountains be carried into the midst of the sea; though the waters thereof roar and be troubled, though the mountains shake with the swelling thereof.' "—GC 638, 639.

"The voice of God is heard from heaven, declaring the day and hour of Jesus' coming, and delivering the everlasting covenant to His people. Like peals of loudest thunder His words roll through the earth. The Israel of God stand listening, with their eyes fixed upward. Their countenances are lighted up with His glory, and shine as did the face of Moses when he came down from Sinai.

The wicked cannot look upon them. And when the blessing is pronounced on those who have honored God by keeping His Sabbath holy, there is a mighty shout of victory.

THE GLORIOUS CLOUD THAT SURROUNDS THE PRINCE OF LIFE

"Soon there appears in the east a small black cloud, about half the size of a man's hand. It is the cloud which surrounds the Saviour and which seems in the distance to be shrouded in darkness. The people of God know this to be the sign of the Son of man. In solemn silence they gaze upon it as it draws nearer the earth, becoming lighter and more glorious, until it is a great white cloud, its base a glory like consuming fire, and above it the rainbow of the covenant. Jesus rides forth as a mighty conqueror. . . . As the living cloud comes still nearer, every eye beholds the Prince of life. . . .

"The righteous cry with trembling: 'Who shall be able to stand?' The angels' song is hushed, and there is a period of awful silence. Then the voice of Jesus is heard, saying: 'My grace is sufficient for you.' The faces of the righteous are lighted up, and joy fills every heart. And the angels strike a note higher and sing again as they draw still nearer to the earth."—GC 640, 641.

CHAPTER 12

FROM THE LIBERATION TO
THE SECOND COMING OF CHRIST

THIS CHAPTER embraces one of the most dramatic periods, and one filled with intense interest—the climax of the agelong conflict.

The main objective of this volume has been to urge the necessity of preparation for this final hour. We will not, therefore, reproduce here the extensive and inspiring descriptions of events traced by the pen of inspiration which crowd into the short period between the liberation and Christ's second coming. They appear in clearly defined chronological order in *The Great Controversy* and in *Early Writings*. We shall, however, make a recapitulation, in outline form, of these tremendous events. In order to present the whole picture, we include here also the happenings described in the previous chapter.

The pertinent spirit of prophecy pages which give the sequence are the following:

　　a. *The Great Controversy*, pages 635-661.

　　b. *Early Writings*, pages 285-291.

RECAPITULATION OF EVENTS

1. **Simultaneous movement to destroy the people of God**
   * It is resolved to make the stroke in one set night.
   * Multitudes of evil men, uttering shouts, will be on the point of rushing upon their prey.
   * They are halted in the act.
     —Dense clouds.
     —A rainbow which reflects the glory of God.
     —The sun appears.

2. **The voice of God: "Look up," and "It is done"**

158

3. Succession of signs and wonders

- Rivers cease to run.
- Black, heavy clouds are parted.
- From a space of indescribable glory comes the voice of God which shakes the heavens and the earth.
- A great earthquake.
    - *—The heavens seem to open and close.*
    - *—Mountains move, rocks are broken off.*
    - *—The sea is lashed into fury.*
    - *—The hurricane shrieks.*
    - *—The whole earth heaves and swells, and its surface breaks up.*
    - *—Inhabited islands disappear.*
    - *—Seaports are swallowed by waves.*
- Hail makes terrible destruction.
- The proudest cities are laid low; palaces fall in ruin.
- Prison walls are rent and the children of God are liberated.

4. A partial resurrection; those who participate—

- All those who died in the faith of the third angel's message.
- Those who mocked Christ.
- Herod.
- Those who smote Him and spit upon Him.
- Those who nailed Him to the cross.
- Many of the scribes and Pharisees.

5. A brilliant star shines through a rift in the clouds

- Hope and joy for the faithful, who shout, "God is our refuge."
- Severity to the transgressors.

6. A hand appears in the sky holding the tables of stone

- All can read them.
- Horror and despair seize those who have trampled upon the precepts of the law.
- All recognize too late the sanctity of the Sabbath.

7. Enemies of God's law suffer results of their unfaithfulness

(Details of this item, briefly referred to in the sequence on page 640 of *The Great Controversy*, are given on pages 654 to 656.)

- They are filled with sorrow, but not repentance.
- No language can describe their despair.
- They accuse each other.
- They heap contempt upon the false shepherds of the flock who have deceived them.
- They pronounce the most dreadful curses against the false shepherds.
- They arise to destroy them. "The swords which were to slay God's people are now employed to destroy their enemies. Everywhere there is strife and bloodshed."
- The angels of death of Ezekiel 9:1-6 do their work.

8. The voice of God proclaims the day and the hour of Christ's coming

9. A small black cloud appears; it envelops the Saviour

- It becomes brighter as it approaches the earth.
- It surrounds the Prince of life, whose countenance outshines the dazzling brightness of the noonday sun.
- Christ descends wrapped in flaming fire.

10. The heavens are rolled together as a scroll, the earth trembles, and the mountains and islands are moved

- The captains, the strong, every bondman, and every freeman hide themselves and call for the rocks to fall upon them.
- From the mouths of the wicked bursts the cry, "The great day of His wrath is come; and who shall be able to stand?"

11. The resurrection of the righteous

- Amid the commotions which engulf the world, Christ calls the righteous dead to life: "Awake!"

- The whole earth rings beneath the tread of the exceeding great multitude who advance clothed with immortal glory. They unite their voices with those of the living saints in a prolonged shout of victory.

12. *The living righteous are transformed and glorified*

13. *Both groups are caught up to meet the Lord in the air*

14. *Those wicked still living are destroyed by the brightness of His coming* (See GC 657.)

15. *Christ confers upon His followers the emblems of victory and covers them with the insignia of royal dignity*
    - Upon the heads of the victors Jesus places with His own right hand the crown of glory.

16. *Jesus opens the pearly gates of the Holy City, and the redeemed enter*
    - Before the throne, on the sea of glass, stands the company of those who have gained the victory over the beast, his image, and his mark.
    - The 144,000 are found there.
    - We, too, must meet each other on the sea of glass.

CHAPTER 13

PREPARATION FOR THE CRISIS

*Introductory note—Seriousness of the time and necessity for
a preparation—Factors in the preparation.*

INTRODUCTORY NOTE

THE THEME of this final chapter is of vital importance. Without doubt, a mere theoretical knowledge of the tremendous events that characterize the last days of the history of our world will not benefit us very much if we do not have an experience of repentance and confession and of cleansing from sin. We must achieve victory over our weaknesses; we must experience complete deliverence by God; and we must demonstrate consecrated activity in giving to the world the message it needs.

The necessity of preparing for the final crisis is so vital that we would be justified in giving here many paragraphs of comment. However, limitations of space prevent extended treatment.

Let us therefore transcribe a few pertinent comments from the pen of inspiration and call the attention of the reader to them. We pray that the Holy Spirit may move each one to take the steps that will draw him closer to heaven and fit him to receive the seal of the living God. This alone can prepare one to pass unharmed through the terrible time of trouble and at last to meet Christ in peace at His second coming.

SERIOUSNESS OF THE TIME AND NECESSITY FOR A PREPARATION

In Matthew 25:5 we read that *all the virgins slept*. The difference between the two groups consisted in the nature of the previous preparation. The wise also slept, but they had entered

162

beforehand into a vital experience with God. They had the oil of the Holy Spirit. The foolish lacked this vital condition for salvation.

The ten virgins represent the church of the last days. All members believe the same truths and wait for the same Lord. But not all are preparing themselves for this most glorious event. Those who will not prepare, will not receive the latter rain. They will be like the foolish virgins. They have the same sincere desire as the wise, but they lack preparation. Many counsels have been written to show the church its great need:

"The 'time of trouble, such as never was,' is soon to open upon us; and we shall need an experience which we do not now possess and which many are too indolent to obtain."—GC 622.

"My brethren, do you realize that your own salvation, as well as the destiny of other souls, depends upon the preparation you now make for the trial before us? Have you that intensity of zeal, that piety and devotion, which will enable you to stand when opposition shall be brought against you? If God has ever spoken by me, the time will come when you will be brought before councils, and every position of truth which you hold will be severely criticized. The time that so many are now allowing to go to waste should be devoted to the charge that God has given us of preparing for the approaching crisis."—5T 716, 717 (2TT 324).

"I saw that God's people are on the enchanted ground, and that some have lost nearly all sense of the shortness of time and the worth of the soul."—EW 120.

"The people need to be aroused in regard to the dangers of the present time. The watchmen are asleep."—5T 715 (2TT 322).

"Satan is marshaling his hosts; and are we individually prepared for the fearful conflict that is just before us? Are we preparing our children for the great crisis?"—*The Adventist Home*, page 186.

"The season of distress and anguish before us will require a faith that can endure weariness, delay, and hunger—a faith that will not faint though severely tried."—GC 621.

"The Lord will have a people as true as steel, and with faith as firm as the granite rock. They are to be His witnesses in the world, His instrumentalities to do a special, a glorious work in the day of His preparation."—4T 594, 595 (1TT 590).

"We should, therefore, be drawing nearer and nearer to the Lord and be earnestly seeking that preparation necessary to enable us to stand in the battle in the day of the Lord. Let all remember that God

is holy and that none but holy beings can ever dwell in His presence."
—EW 71.

"Finally, my brethren, be strong in the Lord, and in the power
of His might. Put on the whole armor of God, that ye may be
able to stand against the wiles of the devil. For we wrestle not
against flesh and blood, but against principalities, against powers,
against the rulers of the darkness of this world, against spiritual
wickedness in high places. Wherefore take unto you the whole
armor of God, that ye may be able to withstand in the evil day,
and having done all, to stand." Ephesians 6:10-13.

"Those who come up to every point, and stand every test, and
overcome, be the price what it may, have heeded the counsel of the
True Witness, and they will receive the latter rain, and thus be fitted
for translation."—1TT 187 (1TT 65).

"I saw that many were neglecting the preparation so needful and
were looking to the time of 'refreshing' and the 'latter rain' to fit them
to stand in the day of the Lord and to live in His sight. Oh, how
many I saw in the time of trouble without a shelter! They had
neglected the needful preparation; therefore they could not receive
the refreshing that all must have to fit them to live in the sight of a
holy God. . . . I saw that none could share the 'refreshing' unless
they obtain the victory over every besetment, over pride, selfishness,
love of the world, and over every wrong word and action."—EW 71.

"We need to humble ourselves before the Lord, with fasting and
prayer, and to meditate much upon His Word, especially upon the
scenes of the judgment."—GC 601.

"Those who make no decided effort, but simply wait for the
Holy Spirit to compel them to action, will perish in darkness. You
are not to sit still and do nothing in the work of God."—ChS 228.

FACTORS IN THE PREPARATION

1. Study of the Bible and the spirit of prophecy

"I have been shown that many who profess to have a knowledge
of present truth know not what they believe. They do not understand the evidences of their faith. They have no just appreciation of
the work for the present time. When the time of trial shall come,
there are men now preaching to others who will find, upon examining
the positions they hold, that there are many things for which they
can give no satisfactory reason. Until thus tested they knew not their
great ignorance. And there are many in the church who take it for

granted that they understand what they believe; but, until controversy arises, they do not know their own weakness. When separated from those of like faith and compelled to stand singly and alone to explain their belief, they will be surprised to see how confused are their ideas of what they had accepted as truth."—5T 707 (2TT 312).

"Those who would stand in this time of peril must understand for themselves the testimony of the Scriptures."—GC 559.

"Those who are earnestly seeking a knowledge of the truth and are striving to purify their souls through obedience, thus doing what they can to prepare for the conflict, will find, in the God of truth, a sure defense."—GC 560.

"Only those who have been diligent students of the Scriptures and who have received the love of the truth will be shielded from the powerful delusion that takes the world captive."—GC 625.

"When the testing time shall come, those who have made God's Word their rule of life will be revealed. In summer there is no noticeable difference between evergreens and other trees; but when the blasts of winter come, the evergreens remain unchanged, while other trees are stripped of their foliage."—GC 602.

"None but those who have fortified the mind with the truths of the Bible will stand through the last great conflict. . . . The decisive hour is even now at hand."—GC 593, 594.

" 'Search the Scriptures.' Study your Bible as you have never studied it before. Unless you arise to a higher, holier state in your religious life, you will not be ready for the appearing of our Lord."—5T 717 (2TT 324).

"As we near the close of this world's history, the prophecies relating to the last days especially demand our study."—COL 133.

"God's Spirit has illuminated every page of Holy Writ, but there are those upon whom it makes little impression, because it is imperfectly understood."—TM 112.

"When God sends to men warnings so important that they are represented as proclaimed by holy angels flying in the midst of heaven, He requires every person endowed with reasoning powers to heed the message. The fearful judgments denounced against the worship of the beast and his image (Revelation 14:9-11), should lead all to a diligent study of the prophecies to learn what the mark of the beast is, and how they are to avoid receiving it."—GC 594.

"So in the prophecies the future is opened before us as plainly as it was opened to the disciples by the words of Christ. The events connected with the close of probation and the work of preparation for the time of trouble, are clearly presented. But multitudes have no more understanding of these important truths than if they had never been revealed. Satan watches to catch away every impression that would make them wise unto salvation, and the time of trouble will find them unready."—GC 594.

"Perilous times are before us. Everyone who has a knowledge of the truth should awake and place himself, body, soul, and spirit, under the discipline of God. The enemy is on our track. We must be wide awake, on our guard against him. We must put on the whole armor of God. We must follow the directions given through the spirit of prophecy. We must love and obey the truth for this time. This will save us from accepting strong delusions. God has spoken to us through His Word. He has spoken to us through the testimonies to the church and through the books that have helped to make plain our present duty and the position that we should now occupy. The warnings that have been given, line upon line, precept upon precept, should be heeded. If we disregard them, what excuse can we offer?"—8T 298 (3TT 275).

"Many are going directly contrary to the light which God has given to His people, because they do not read the books which contain the light and knowledge in cautions, reproofs, and warnings."—4T 391.

Note that incomplete comprehension of the truths and divine prophecies, both of the Bible and of the spirit of prophecy, results from lack of diligent study accompanied by prayer.

2. Communion with God; fervent prayer

"As the praying ones continued their earnest cries, at times a ray of light from Jesus came to them, to encourage their hearts and light up their countenances. Some, I saw, did not participate in this work of agonizing and pleading. They seemed indifferent and careless. They were not resisting the darkness around them, and it shut them in like a thick cloud. The angels of God left these and went to the aid of the earnest, praying ones. I saw angels of God hasten to the assistance of all who were struggling with all their power to resist the evil angels and trying to help themselves by calling upon God with perseverance. But His angels left those who made no effort to help themselves, and I lost sight of them."—EW 270.

"They should make mighty intercession with God for help now. The love of Christ must be diffused in their own hearts. The Spirit of Christ must be poured out upon them, and they must be making ready to stand in the judgment."—5T 454 (2TT 154).

It is necessary for us to watch and pray with the same fervor that Jacob exercised in his night of trouble. Only when we strive in this manner with God will our lives be transformed and our filthy rags exchanged for the robe of Christ's righteousness. Finally, as a result of our obtaining this necessary preparation, our names also will be changed.

3. Cleansing from sin and victory over weaknesses

"Had not Jacob previously repented of his sin in obtaining the birthright by fraud, God would not have heard his prayer and mercifully preserved his life. So, in the time of trouble, if the people of God had unconfessed sins to appear before them while tortured with fear and anguish, they would be overwhelmed. . . .

"Satan leads many to believe that God will overlook their unfaithfulness in the minor affairs of life; but the Lord shows in His dealings with Jacob that He will in no wise sanction or tolerate evil. All who endeavor to excuse or conceal their sins, and permit them to remain upon the books of heaven, unconfessed and unforgiven, will be overcome by Satan."—GC 620.

"In view of that great day the Word of God, in the most solemn and impressive language, calls upon His people to arouse from their spiritual lethargy and to seek His face with repentance and humiliation: 'Blow ye the trumpet in Zion, and sound an alarm in My holy mountain.' "—GC 311.

"Therefore also now, saith the Lord, turn ye even to Me with all your heart, and with fasting, and with weeping, and with mourning." Joel 2:12.

"Those who receive the seal of the living God and are protected in the time of trouble must reflect the image of Jesus fully."—EW 71.

"Not one of us will ever receive the seal of God while our characters have one spot or stain upon them. It is left with us to remedy the defects in our characters, to cleanse the soul temple of every defilement. Then the latter rain will fall upon us as the early rain fell upon the disciples on the Day of Pentecost."—5T 214 (2TT 69).

"Said the angel: 'God will bring His work closer and closer to test and prove every one of His people.' Some are willing to receive one point; but when God brings them to another testing point, they shrink from it and stand back, because they find that it strikes directly at some cherished idol. Here they have opportunity to see what is in their hearts that shuts out Jesus. They prize something higher than the truth, and their hearts are not prepared to receive Jesus. Individuals are tested and proved a length of time to see if they will sacrifice their idols and heed the counsel of the True Witness."—1T 187 (1TT 64, 65).

4. *A complete surrender to God*

"When the soul surrenders itself to Christ, a new power takes possession of the new heart. A change is wrought which man can never accomplish for himself. It is a supernatural work, bringing a supernatural element into human nature. The soul that is yielded to Christ becomes His own fortress, which He holds in a revolted world, and He intends that no authority shall be known in it but His own. A soul thus kept in possession by the heavenly agencies is impregnable to the assaults of Satan."—DA 324.

"Consecrate yourself to God in the morning; make this your very first work. Let your prayer be, 'Take me, O Lord, as wholly Thine. I lay all my plans at Thy feet. Use me today in Thy service. Abide with me, and let all my work be wrought in Thee.' This is a daily matter. Each morning consecrate yourself to God for that day. Surrender all your plans to Him, to be carried out or given up as His providence shall indicate. Thus day by day you may be giving your life into the hands of God, and thus your life will be molded more and more after the life of Christ."—SC 70.

Our surrender to Christ, our consecration to God, in order to be effective, must be renewed each day.

"Satan does not want anyone to see the necessity of an entire surrender to God. When the soul fails to make this surrender, sin is not forsaken; the appetites and passions are striving for the mastery; temptations confuse the conscience, so that true conversion does not take place. If all had a sense of the conflict which each soul must wage with satanic agencies that are seeking to ensnare, entice, and deceive, there would be much more diligent labor for those who are young in the faith."—6T 92, 93 (2TT 390).

5. *A diligent work for Christ*

"We are to be as men waiting for their Lord, not in idle expectancy, but in earnest work, with unwavering faith. It is no time now to allow our minds to be engrossed with things of minor importance."—5T 452 (2TT 152).

"The work which the church has failed to do in a time of peace and prosperity she will have to do in a terrible crisis under most discouraging, forbidding circumstances. The warnings that worldly conformity has silenced or withheld must be given under the fiercest opposition from enemies of the faith."—5T 463 (2TT 164).

"We have no time to lose. The end is near. The passage from place to place to spread the truth will soon be hedged with dangers on the right hand and on the left. Everything will be placed to obstruct the way of the Lord's messengers, so that they will not be able to do that which it is possible for them to do now. We must look our work fairly in the face and advance as fast as possible in aggressive warfare."—6T 22 (2TT 375, 376).

"Christ has committed to your trust talents of means and of influence, and He has said to you: Improve these till I come. When the Master cometh and reckoneth with His servants, and all are called to the strictest account as to how they have used the talents entrusted to them, how will you, my dear brother, bear the investigation?"—4T 51.

6. *Activity on behalf of religious liberty*

"It is our duty to do all in our power to avert the threatened danger. We should endeavor to disarm prejudice by placing ourselves in a proper light before the people. We should bring before them the real question at issue, thus interposing the most effectual protest against measures to restrict liberty of conscience. We should search the Scriptures and be able to give the reason for our faith. Says the prophet: 'The wicked shall do wickedly: and none of the wicked shall understand; but the wise shall understand.' "—5T 452 (2TT 152).

"When the National Reformers began to urge measures to restrict religious liberty, our leading men should have been alive to the situation and should have labored earnestly to counteract these efforts. It is not in the order of God that light has been kept from our people —the very present truth which they needed for this time. Not all our ministers who are giving the third angel's message really understand what constitutes that message. The National Reform movement has been regarded by some as of so little importance that they have not thought it necessary to give much attention to it and have even felt that in so doing they would be giving time to questions distinct from the third angel's message."—5T 715 (2TT 321, 322).

This paragraph and the following one refer to an endeavor during the late 1880's to declare the United States a Christian nation and to revise the Constitution, thus abrogating to a large extent the separation of church and state.

"But too often the leader has stood hesitating, seeming to say: 'Let us not be in too great haste. There may be a mistake. We must be careful not to raise a false alarm.' The very hesitancy and uncertainty on his part is crying: ' "Peace and safety." Do not get excited. Be not alarmed. There is a great deal more made of this religious amendment question than is demanded. This agitation will all die down.' Thus he virtually denies the message sent from God, and the warning which was designed to stir the churches fails to do its work."—5T 715, 716 (2TT 322).

"We as a people have not accomplished the work which God has committed to us. We are not ready for the issue to which the enforcement of the Sunday law will bring us. It is our duty, as we see the signs of approaching peril, to arouse to action. Let none sit in calm expectation. . . . Let there be most earnest prayer, and then let us work in harmony with our prayers."—5T 713, 714 (2TT 320, 321).

May God help us, as His people, to comprehend the seriousness of the time in which we live. May He help us to see our great spiritual deficiency and cause us to seek with all our hearts a true experience with God. Such an experience will fit us to pass triumphantly through the final hours of trial and meet the Lord in peace.

EPILOGUE

THE PAGES of this book have brought before us, largely from inspired teachings, outstanding events which are to agitate the world and shake the church of God during the final hours of probation and on through the time of trouble.

We have observed how the Spirit of God produces a spiritual reformation within the church, augmented by the preaching of the message of the Faithful Witness to Laodicea, and illuminated by the great topic of righteousness by faith.

The survey has shown us the sealing work, giving us some idea of the gravity of the hour in which we live. It has cheered us with a preview of great miracles to be wrought under the latter rain, when the gospel shall be proclaimed with marvelous results, rising to a crescendo with the loud cry of the angel of Revelation 18.

The sad experience of the sifting has been set before us, alerting us to the danger which we all face unless we are firmly grounded on the immovable Rock of Ages and thoroughly familiar with divine truth.

We have seen ominous but real scenes of persecution looming ahead, soon to be started by Sunday legislation. Enacted first in the United States and later in all other countries, these laws will eventually carry the death penalty. But the dark panorama spread before us was immediately illuminated by the wonderful promises of God's protection and final deliverance. In the climactic moment of Christ's appearing in glory, which paralyzes the wicked and liberates the righteous, we beheld in prospect the magnificent spectacle which will crown our millennial hopes with triumph.

Assurance that angels will assist the faithful and that extraordinary manifestations of the goodness of God will sustain them during the time of trouble and the falling of the plagues has renewed in us sentiments of gratitude to our loving heavenly Father.

The rapid unfolding of events in the fields of science, politics, economics, morality, and religion, portrayed daily by press, radio, and television, overwhelms us today with evidence that we are living in earth's last hours, that the sun of grace and mercy is about to set forever, and that the short night which precedes the glorious morning will soon commence.

Side by side with this observation comes a challenge—the possibility of doing a short but glorious work of final witnessing under an extraordinary display of divine power. This stimulates us to redouble our efforts, multiply our enthusiasm, and dedicate all our resources to the blessed task of finishing the work.

But what if all this catches us unready? Supposing the final hour of the world—or of our own lives—should overtake us as a thief in the night before we have made the necessary spiritual preparation? What value will merely knowing these things be?

The Lord longs for us to shake off our lukewarmness and indifference, giving heed to the counsel of the Faithful Witness. He wants us to dedicate necessary time to Bible study, prayer, and a careful examination of our spiritual problems. He warns us against being satisfied with our own spiritual attainments and admonishes us instead to take hold of the righteousness of Christ and claim the powerful work of His grace in conquering sin in our lives. He would have us overcome our defects and reflect in our lives, always more perfectly, the image of Christ.

God anxiously desires, finally, that we cut all ties between ourselves and the vanities of the world; that we renounce self with its pride and covetousness; and that, learning from the Great Teacher how to be meek and humble of heart, we make a total and unconditional surrender of our lives to Him. Thus the great miracle of victory will be worked in us.

Thus we shall be, by the grace of God, abundantly prepared for the events we expect, and our example will motivate others to make the same preparation. The Lord has made all necessary provisions for our eternal triumph. May He give to each of us the determination to avail ourselves of them, to the end that we may share at last in the eternal reward to be granted to the victorious in the kingdom of glory.

APPENDIX
IMPORTANT EVENTS
THAT FULFILL PROPHECIES

This appendix is a contribution by M. E. LOEWEN, secretary of the Religious Liberty Department of the General Conference.

THE PANORAMA of the events which according to the prophecies will mark the final hours before the second coming of Christ, affords the student a special inspiration. Danger exists that a careless observer may fail to perceive the significance of the incidents taking place before us, considering them as mere products of the normal course of things. Some of these events, nevertheless, become important indications of the fact that certain prophecies of great significance are actually in the process of fulfillment.

Let us notice here, therefore, eleven outstanding statements from the Scriptures and from the spirit of prophecy, and trace the unfolding of their fulfillment in the actual events.

BRIDGING THE GULF

We read in *The Great Controversy*:

"The Protestants of the United States will be foremost in stretching their hands across the gulf to grasp the hand of spiritualism; they will reach over the abyss to clasp hands with the Roman power; and under the influence of this threefold union, this country will follow in the steps of Rome in trampling on the rights of conscience."—Page 588.

Strikingly, Cardinal Cushing, writing a pastoral letter, used the word "gulf" to describe the separating space between Protestantism and Catholicism:

"For the past several centuries there has been either a great silence or a species of embittered argument between us and those

173

who, like us, bear the Christian name. Whether in silence or in recrimination, there has been a great gulf between us. That gulf we set ourselves to bridge."—*Pastoral Letter,* March 6, 1960.

The Rev. Ralph D. Hyslop, professor of ecumenical studies and director of the program of advanced religious studies at Union Theological Seminary, appeared on a panel at an interfaith discussion on church unity at the Protestant Episcopal Church of the Heavenly Rest. He said:

"If indeed Christ gave to Peter and to his successors that kingly authority which is surely His to give, that the head of the church upon earth might have the power to maintain the truth in spite of all error, . . . then it is not safe to resist the loving summons of the Vicar of Christ. . . . May I add that the embodiment of a doctrine in a person is at this moment in history most persuasive in the person of John XXIII."—*Catholic Review,* Feb. 2, 1962.

Methodist Bishop James K. Matthews, president of the Massachusetts Council of Churches, said:

"There is now with an increasingly clear voice being heard across what might have been termed an abyss of separation . . . the cry, 'Brother,' and that's a cry that has been directed from both sides, and we find that abyss perhaps isn't as broad or as deep as was supposed."—*Liberty,* May-June, 1963, page 22.

The final objective of Catholicism is to effect total unification, and receive the Protestants back into the fold as full-fledged Roman Catholics. Note the words of Father Francis J. Cornell, a theologian of the Catholic University of America:

"Good fellowship and friendliness among all Christians are indeed helpful as an intermediate step, but the final object of ecumenism, as Catholics conceive it, is unity in faith, worship, and the acknowledgment of the supreme spiritual authority of the Bishop of Rome. In the words of Cardinal Bea: 'The Council's main ecumenical task will be to prepare for eventual union, God willing, by bettering relations between Catholics and non-Catholics.' And Pope John XXIII, addressing those separated from Rome, said: 'May we hope with a father's love for your return.' Honesty demands that we let our separated brethren know that this is our ultimate reason for participating in the ecumenical movement, and that we manifest it in practice by seeking to convert even devout Protestants."—Quoted in an editorial of *Christian Heritage,* June, 1964, page 5.

An unusual suggestion, but entirely within the meaning of the prophecy regarding a union between the Protestants and Rome, is that of Dr. Tamburro, of the Protestant Episcopal Church. *Religious News Service* reports:

"An Episcopal minister has suggested that Richard Cardinal Cushing, Roman Catholic Archbishop of Boston, should be invited to fill the post which will become vacant upon the resignation of Presiding Bishop Arthur Lichtenberger of the Protestant Episcopal Church.

"The Rev. Wendell B. Tamburro, rector of the Church of the Holy Innocents, Highlands Falls, N.Y., made his suggestion in a 'Letter to the Editor' of *The Living Church* (May 17), Episcopal weekly published here.

"Noting that Bishop Lichtenberger's unfortunate resignation for reasons of health 'poses a problem for the church,' the rector stated, 'I would like to see someone [in authority] propose to the forthcoming General Convention that it might strike out in faith and invite Richard Cardinal Cushing to be Presiding Bishop.'

"The minister allowed that 'if, through the leading of the Holy Spirit,' Cardinal Cushing accepted, 'this would be the greatest breakthrough in the ecclesiastical "lace-cotta wall" in generations.' . . .

"He noted that such a 'breakthrough' would require the permission of Pope Paul VI and revision of Episcopal canon law."—May 19, 1964.

Surely the inspired words, "And all the world wondered after the beast," are being implemented in this our day.

When you are considering "bridging the gulf," include this item:

"Philadelphia, Pa.—A book underscoring differences between Catholics and Lutherans has been canceled by the twenty-one-member board of parish education of the United Lutheran Church.

"It was explained that at the time the book was authorized there were marked differences which have been quieted by 'conversations between the two faiths and upon understanding each other.' "—*Catholic Review,* Jan. 1, 1962.

Can your imagination picture what Martin Luther's reaction would have been to such a conclusion? The differences have been "quieted"!

Or consider this item taken from the wires of United Press International:

"Castel Gandolfo, Italy, August 18, 1964—Pope Paul VI yesterday received in audience Moderator Elder G. Hawkins of the United Presbyterian Church of the United States.

"Hawkins, first Negro ever to hold the moderator's post, was accompanied by the Rev. Dr. Eugene Carson Blake, stated clerk of the United Presbyterian's General Assembly, and Richard L. Davies, chairman of the Presbyterian Committee on Ecumenical Relations.

"At the end of the audience the pope and the visiting Presbyterians recited the Lord's Prayer together.

"One by one the religious leaders in the Protestant world connected with the World Council of Churches and the ecumenical movement are making their way to Rome. . . .

"First, the broad inclusivism accepted by modern Protestantism makes possible the inclusion of the Roman Catholic Church. Second, the subordination of Scripture to the will of the church has moved liberal Protestantism over onto the same platform as Roman Catholicism so far as the doctrine of the church is concerned."—*Christian Beacon*, Thursday, August 27, 1964, a weekly newspaper.

CATHOLICISM DOES NOT CHANGE

"It is not without reason that the claim has been put forth in Protestant countries that Catholicism differs less widely from Protestantism than in former times. There has been a change; but the change is not in the papacy. Catholicism indeed resembles much of the Protestantism that now exists, because Protestantism has so greatly degenerated since the days of the Reformers."—GC 571.

A secular newsmagazine will give us a glimpse into the situation as Catholics and the world analyze it.

"Catholic theologians are looking upon Protestant theologians with a new friendliness and respect. The change reflects much more than an increase of tolerance, it is rather a consequence of the change that has taken place within Protestantism, change which, on the one hand, leads Protestant theology closer to the tradition of the church, and, on the other, offers, by its profundity, a true challenge to Catholic theology."—*Time,* May 30, 1960, quoted from *Commonweal,* Catholic weekly.

A leading Catholic theologian gives his opinion of the possibility of any change in Catholic belief to facilitate the return of the "separated brethren":

"If Catholicism drops . . . the dogma of her own exclusive function to mediate between God and man, . . . she certainly would be no longer Catholic.

"For ecumenical work the Catholic can follow only one tactic. He must ask the Protestant to be converted to Catholicism."—Father Gustave Weigel, S.J., Woodstock College, *An American Dialogue,* New York, Doubleday & Co., Inc., 1961, pages 218, 220.

The attitude of the hierarchy is expressed forcefully in *Our Sunday Visitor:*

"Protestantism is just as wrong now as it was in 1517. It is the duty incumbent on us as Catholics to 'spread the word' and make America Catholic. . . . Father Isaac Hecker founded the Paulist Fathers for the express purpose of 'making America Catholic.' They are still at it and doing a fine job of it. It is the goal of every bishop, priest, and religious order in the country. No Catholic can settle, with good conscience, for a policy of appeasement, or even mere coexistence with a non-Catholic community." —July 31, 1960.

Ellen G. White pointed out long ago this attitude of conformity that would exist on the part of Protestants:

"Romanism is now regarded by Protestants with far greater favor than in former years. . . . There is an increasing indifference concerning the doctrines that separate the reformed churches from the papal hierarchy; the opinion is gaining ground that, after all, we do not differ so widely upon vital points as has been supposed, and that a little concession on our part will bring us into a better understanding with Rome."—GC 563.

Augustin Cardinal Bea, president of the Vatican Secretariat for Promoting Christian Unity, said at Harvard University, in March, 1963:

"The Roman Catholic Church would be gravely misunderstood if it should be concluded that her present ecumenical adventuresomeness and openness meant that she was prepared to reexamine any of her fixed dogmatic positions. What the church is prepared to do is to take the responsibility for a more imaginative and contemporary presentation of these fixed positions."—Quoted in *Church and State*, December, 1963.

REPUDIATION OF THE CONSTITUTION

"When . . . our country shall repudiate every principle of its Constitution as a Protestant and republican government, and shall make provision for the propagation of papal falsehoods and delusions, then we may know that the time has come for the marvelous working of Satan and that the end is near."—5T 451.

The following could be an isolated case of the negation of American and democratic principles. Nevertheless it is an indication of deep-seated feelings which are generally held. The author, a Jesuit, points out the fact that the American Constitution is relatively recent and that it is not sufficiently tested:

"I just don't understand the reverence, not to say adoration, which everybody here seems to pay to the 'Amuricun Constitooshun.' I want to hear some American get up and shout: 'Give us justice. Give us decency. And to hell with the American Constitution!'

"After all, the American Constitution, though a most respectable document, was composed at a particular period in history—and that only 180 years or so ago. I have talked with the Lord North whose grandfather tried to suppress the American rebels. The night before I flew from London, I slept in an Augustinian monastery built in 1248. Perhaps for this reason I don't attach so great importance to things only a couple of centuries old."—Father Bernard Leeming, S.J., *The Catholic News*, Thursday, July 25, 1963.

This outburst is occasioned by the desire to receive Government money for church (Catholic) schools. One is disconcerted when he realizes the implacable drive of the Roman Catholic Church for state funds. The hierarchy approaches the matter with confidence that such funds are theirs by natural right and that they will receive them. The presumptuous assurance of the superiority of the Roman Catholic Church is constantly evident.

Whenever the Roman Catholic discusses state aid for his schools, an intolerant disregard for present constitutional barriers cannot be suppressed. It is not difficult to detect his impatience with and scorn for the conscientious feelings of others who may differ with him. This spirit could spark the forces that will eventually repudiate the principles of the Constitution.

It is with awe that we realize how exactly this attitude fits the picture boldly revealed in prophecies for our day.

STATE SUPPORT FOR CHURCH INSTITUTIONS

Another declaration from the spirit of prophecy causes us to consider the approval and the support which the state offers to the church and its doctrines. Turning to *The Great Controversy,* we read the following:

"In the movements now in progress in the United States to secure for the institutions and usages of the church the support of the state, Protestants are following in the steps of papists. Nay, more, they are opening the door for the papacy to regain in Protestant America the supremacy which she has lost in the Old World." —Page 573.

The decision of the Supreme Court of the United States that Sunday laws are within the province of the secular power is one step in the fulfillment of this passage.

While the word "institutions" refers more specifically to the laws and teachings of the church, such as the reverence for the first day of the week, yet there is an application to various facilities the church employs to do her work.

December 10, 1963, there was enacted into law a provision for educational institutions to receive grants and loans of Federal tax money. The fund established one billion two hundred million dollars for this purpose. These funds are also available to church-affiliated colleges to erect buildings for nonreligious purposes on their campuses.

At the present time it appears that the greatest drive to destroy the separation of church and state will be motivated by the desire for state funds by church officials.

In 1963, Mr. Justice Douglas said in his concurring opinion in the Abington v. Schempp case:

"The most effective way to establish any institution is to finance it; and this truth is reflected in the appeals by church groups for public funds to finance their religious schools. Financing a church either in its strictly religious activities or in its other activities is equally unconstitutional, as I understand the Establishment Clause. The allusion here is to the First Amendment of the Constitution of the United States, which says, among other things: 'Congress shall make no law respecting an establishment of religion, or prohibiting the free exercise thereof.' This amendment forms a part of the Bill of Rights which was put in force in 1791. Budgets for one activity may be technically separable from budgets for others. But the institution is an inseparable whole, a living organism, which is strengthened in proselytizing when it is strengthened in any department by contributions from other than its own members."

While still president of Brigham Young University in Provo, Utah, Dr. Ernest L. Wilkinson turned down Federal funds for the university that would have totaled $3,750,000 during a period of five years. Let us hope that more church educators will have the courage to refuse Caesar's tax money.

SUNDAY LAWS DISGUISED

Prophecy:

"The Sunday movement is now making its way in darkness. The leaders are concealing the true issue, and many who unite in the movement do not themselves see whither the undercurrent is tending."—5T 452.

On May 29, 1961, the Supreme Court of the United States decided that Sunday laws are constitutional. In an outstanding manner, an associate justice of the Supreme Court of the United States is made to echo the words of the servant of God in order to state his dissenting to the opinion of the court on Sunday laws:

"For in his case the Court seems to say, without so much as a deferential nod toward that high place which we have accorded religious freedom in the past, that any substantial interest will justify encroachments on religious practice, at least if those encroachments are cloaked in the guise of some nonreligious public purpose."—Justice Brennan, Braunfield v. Brown, May 29, 1961.

In the spirit of prophecy we read "darkness," "concealing," and in the opinion of a Justice of the Supreme Court we hear the echo, "cloaked," "guise." Certainly this is a startling repetition of an idea by two individuals who had no opportunity for collusion.

Dr. Melvin Forney, formerly executive secretary of the Lord's Day Alliance, wrote in the official paper of the Alliance, *Lord's Day Leader:*

"The third challenge comes from within the Christian church. There is a small number of ministers and other Christian leaders who . . . feel that we do not have the right to impose our day of worship upon another. They state that the observance of worship is a matter of conscience and should be left to our conscience. This group within the church, even though it is small, gives real cause for alarm."

Dr. Forney here emphasizes the religious value of Sunday legislation. Later, when asked why his organization had not presented this argument before the Supreme Court when the Sunday-law cases were being considered, Dr. Forney wrote:

"As an organization we refrained from filing a friend of the court brief . . . because we felt it wise to present the argument on behalf of the Lord's Day as a matter of civil law instead of on a religious basis."—March, 1961.

So Sunday laws are being argued as a health and welfare measure and the true issue is being concealed. Chief Justice Warren admitted that Sunday laws had their origin in religion but argued that today they are merely secular measures. Mr. Justice Douglas disagreed and contended that Sunday laws will always be religious because of their origin.

Dr. Samuel Jarnes, who at the time was the executive secretary for the New Jersey Lord's Day Alliance, wrote an article entitled "Never on Sunday" for the *Christianity Today* of October 26, 1962. Though his organization has repeatedly emphasized the value of Sunday legislation to protect the sanctity of Sunday, his first sentence in this article was: "It should be determined, once for all, that Sunday laws in our nation are not religious laws."

To point out the lack of reasoning in Dr. Jarnes's statement I answered him and wrote in part:

"It is argued that Sunday laws are no longer religious laws. No amount of camouflage can obliterate the religious significance of Sunday laws. Though Jacob covered his arms with sheepskin and donned Esau's clothing, it did not change his voice nor the fact of his birth. Likewise, no secular disguise can conceal the religious origin of Sunday laws with their historical roots in sixteen hundred years of religious legislation, nor muffle the voice of religious bigotry with which they speak."

Labor unions, chambers of commerce, and merchants' associations have been deceived into believing that Sunday laws are merely secular regulatory measures. And that is precisely what the prophecy foretold.

PROCLAMATION OF THE SABBATH TRUTH

Someone may ask: Since the Scriptures foretell Sunday laws, since the spirit of prophecy has clearly outlined the passage of Sunday laws in these last days, why should Seventh-day Adventists oppose these laws? Are not these tactics delaying the fulfillment of prophecy? Why not work for stringent Sunday laws, the stricter the better? Are Seventh-day Adventists working in harmony with God's will when they oppose that which He has said will come to pass? Why does the Lord permit Sunday laws anyway?

The servant of God answers:

"The Lord in His providence is far ahead of us. He has permitted this Sunday question to be pressed to the front, that the Sabbath of the fourth commandment may be presented before the legislative assemblies; thus the leading men of the nation may have their attention called to the testimony of God's Word in favor of the true Sabbath. If it does not convert them, it is a witness to condemn."—MS 16, 1890.

The governor of Massachusetts appointed a commission to review the antiquated Sunday laws of that state. Pastor Merle Mills, president of the Southern New England Conference, was one of those appointed to this commission. At the first meeting each member told his position toward Sunday laws. At the close of that meeting one of the men rushed up to Pastor Mills and taking him by the arm said very earnestly, "Where do you fellows get the idea that Saturday is the Sabbath day?" And right there a portion of the quotation given above was fulfilled.

The governor of Maryland similarly appointed a commission to study Sunday laws. This commission announced an open meeting for the general public to allow the people to state their convictions regarding Sunday laws. For an entire afternoon speeches were made, some for, some against, Sunday laws. At the close the chairman turned to his colleagues and said: "All afternoon we have heard only one objection to Sunday laws. That is that Sunday laws are religious. Now if we could only get a Sunday law that wasn't religious, we'd have no trouble."

At that point, a gentleman in the rear of the auditorium arose and asked permission to make a statement that would help on that point. Permission was granted, so he came forward and, facing the assembly, he said: "I am the Rev. Frank Brassington, pastor of the Silver Spring Baptist Church. Mr. Chairman, if you want Scripture background for your Sabbath keeping, then I would recommend you go to our Seventh-day Adventist friends. For, Mr. Chairman, you can read your Bible through, and you'll not find one word that sanctifies Sunday as the Sabbath. Therefore, Mr. Chairman, go ahead and pass all the Sunday laws you want, there's nothing sacred about Sunday."

As Sunday hearings are held around the country, it is amazing to learn the number of officials in high places who think that Sunday is the seventh day of the week. According to the statement we are considering, Sunday laws are being agitated to give an opportunity to tell these men about the true Sabbath.

AN OPPORTUNITY FOR EVANGELISM

"Evangelists should be finding their way into all the places where the minds of men are agitated over the question of Sunday legislation and the teaching of religion in the public schools."—9T 51.

The city of Shreveport, Louisiana, held a referendum on a Sunday ordinance. Preceding the election, the Seventh-day Adventists had a number of programs on radio and on TV stating the backgrounds of Sunday legislation and their objections to it.

Two days after the election, a letter was received which read in part as follows: "I am a Sunday School teacher and am very much interested in what you had to say on the television program about the seventh-day Sabbath. My class has been studying the Ten Commandments, and we are trying to find out what is really required. Would it be possible for you to let us know more about your understanding of the fourth commandment? . . . What a tragedy it would be if our Lord found us keeping the wrong day when He returns!"

The pastor visited there and found a group of 135 willing to attend Bible studies every week. A church has been raised up in that community as a result of this interest in the Sunday-law question.

Experiences like this, which are reminiscent of the work of the Holy Spirit in the apostolic church, can be multiplied as our people take advantage of the interest in Sunday legislation.

A RELIGIOUS AMENDMENT TO THE CONSTITUTION

Before the turn of the century there had been a campaign to secure an amendment to the American Constitution declaring this a Christian nation. Referring to this movement in the *Review and Herald,* Mrs. E. G. White wrote:

"An amendment to our Constitution is being urged in Congress, and when it is obtained, oppression must follow. . . . Shall we let this Religious Amendment movement come in, and shut us away from our privileges and rights, because we keep the commandments of God? God help us to arouse from the stupor that has hung over us for years!"—Dec. 18, 1888.

"If the startling transactions taking place in our country today, in regard to the Religious Amendment, had been realized by our people in every church; had they seen the plain, decided fulfillment of prophecy, and aroused to the demands of the crisis, they would not now be under such stupor and deathlike slumber."—*Ibid.*

For more than a generation the religious amendment seemed to be a dead issue. However, since the decisions of the Federal Supreme Court on prayer and Bible reading in the public schools, the drive for a religious amendment to the Constitution has been revived. After the announcement of the court's decision, a hysterical, emotional reaction swept over certain areas of the country.

Though more than 140 bills were introduced into Congress seeking to amend the Constitution, the interest in 1964 centered in what was known as the Becker Amendment.

Mr. Becker went farther in his proposition than to allow prayer and Bible reading in the public schools. The second section of his resolution would amend the Constitution to read as follows:

"SECTION 2. Nothing in this Constitution shall be deemed to prohibit making reference to belief in, reliance upon, or invoking the aid of God or a Supreme Being in any governmental or public document, proceeding, activity, ceremony, school institution, or place, or upon any coinage, currency, or obligation of the United States."

Does the wording "invoking the aid of God . . . in any governmental . . . ceremony" pretend to allow a Roman Catholic mass to be said or even a Protestant evangelistic service to be held at the whim of a Government department?

When Mr. Becker testified before the House Judiciary Committee, he was asked how the prayers would be chosen by the schools. He finally agreed that they should be the responsibility of the local school board. When asked what the parents could do if they didn't approve of the prayer or the version of the Bible used in the school, Mr. Becker replied that they would have the privilege of voting that board out and electing another. In this way, religion would become part of each school-board election. There are 50,454 school districts, so there would be the possibility of more than 50,000 religious battles each election day.

Each teacher would in effect undergo a religious test. He would have to decide whether he could conscientiously recite the prayer required or use the version of the Bible prescribed. Each student would face a similar test as he struggled with his conscience when asked to participate in the religious exercises. Of course, Mr. Becker provided that these prayers must be on a voluntary basis. But the courts in America have stated that the social pressures upon children and the desire for approval from their schoolmates would prevent many children from making a conscientious choice.

RELIGIOUS OBSERVANCES ENFORCED BY LAW

"Let the principle once be established in the United States that the church may employ or control the power of the state; that religious observances may be enforced by secular laws; in short, that the authority of church and state is to dominate the conscience, and the triumph of Rome in this country is assured."—GC 581.

When the Supreme Court considered the Sunday-law cases, it was argued that Sunday laws are religious. In his dissenting opinion Justice Douglas contended they are still religious. In spite of the impressive evidence presented, the court ruled Sunday laws to be secular laws. The weight of law was placed behind the Sunday legislation.

In Massachusetts in 1962 an amendment to the existing Sunday laws would have permitted observers of the seventh day to keep their places of business open on Sunday. This was approved by the State Senate on June 7, 1962, by a vote of twenty-one to fourteen.

Immediately an editorial appeared in the *Pilot*, the Catholic archdiocesan paper, fiercely attacking the senators who voted for this amendment. The names of these senators were printed, and the promise was made that these men would be remembered at the next election. The editorial said, "The senators responded to pressures that will destroy the Sunday observances in favor of those—principally Jews and Adventists—who worship on Saturday." This was a frank admission that the religious motive was predominant.

The next Sunday the Catholics attending services in the Boston area were all urged to contact their senators and urge reconsideration. It was reported that a vicious attack was mounted which became almost unbearable in its intensity.

On Monday morning reconsideration of the amendment was voted, and after a short discussion the measure was killed by a vote of thirty-one to eight.

We have the prophecy before us. Also we face clear evidence that a religious observance could be protected by law. The word is true, and its fulfillment is sure.

CHILDREN OF GOD CALLED ENEMIES OF LAW AND ORDER

"Those who honor the Bible Sabbath will be denounced as enemies of law and order, as breaking down the moral restraints of society, causing anarchy and corruption, and calling down the judgments of God upon the earth. Their conscientious scruples will be pronounced obstinacy, stubbornness, and contempt of authority. They will be accused of disaffection toward the government."—GC 592.

A look at two statements from two church leaders will give us an idea how these words can be fulfilled. First we turn to the words of Cardinal Cushing:

"United States Catholics feel as I do—that the one thing that can save Latin America, even in its relations with this country, is the (Roman) Catholic religion. It is the one bond, shared by all. . . . Some non-Catholic sects such as the Jehovah's Witnesses, the Seventh-day Adventists, and other extremists, are doing immeasurable harm by destroying the faith of the poor people. They are simply making the roadway wider, more attractive, and more accessible for the army of communists."—Richard Cardinal Cushing, quoted in *Sign,* a Catholic magazine, October 1961, page 73.

Then we turn to the words of a Methodist bishop.

"When we give our consent to a wide-open Sunday which becomes as any other day, we copy the program of the atheistic communists and reveal a greater stupidity by approving what they have demonstrated cannot be done."—Bishop Marshall Reed, *The Michigan Christian Advocate,* March 13, 1958.

Perhaps this will serve to emphasize the words of Ellen G. White: "The Protestant world today see in the little company keeping the Sabbath a Mordecai in the gate."—5T 450.

Now let us turn to the last prophecy in this series.

SATAN ATTEMPTS TO MAKE IT IMPOSSIBLE TO KEEP THE SABBATH

The words of Satan are not quoted often, either in the Scriptures or in the spirit of prophecy. Three times in the Bible—in

Eden, during Job's experience, and during the temptation of Christ—are his words recorded. In *Prophets and Kings* Ellen G. White follows the unusual practice of quoting a lengthy statement of Satan's. The following words are taken from this speech:

" 'The world will become mine. I will be the ruler of the earth, the prince of the world. I will so control the minds under my power that God's Sabbath shall be a special object of contempt. A sign? I will make the observance of the seventh day a sign of disloyalty to the authorities of earth. Human laws will be made so stringent that men and women will not dare to observe the seventh-day Sabbath. For fear of wanting food and clothing, they will join with the world in transgressing God's law. The earth will be wholly under my dominion.' "—Page 184.

Of recent date an authoritative voice has been raised to claim that the Roman Catholic Church is responsible for the change of the Sabbath. In his famous encyclical, *"Mater et Magistra,"* Pope John XXIII wrote:

"249. . . . [The Church] has never failed to insist that the third commandment: 'Remember to keep holy the Sabbath day,' be carefully observed by all. . . .

"251. . . . We exhort, as it were, with the words of God Himself, all men, whether public officials or representatives of management and labor, that they observe this command of God Himself and of the Catholic Church, and judge in their souls that they have a responsibility to God and society in this regard."

During the second session of Vatican Council II, on October 25, 1963, an action was taken by the vote of 2,058 to 9, to favor a perpetual calendar which would fix the date of Easter. In *The Christian Century* of November 13, 1963, an editorial on this action of the Council, but particularly favoring the fixing of a date for Easter, said:

"We suggest a world conference of representatives of the various Christian bodies to be held to bring to fruition what Vatican II has made possible."

Two points should be noted. First, again a leader in the Catholic Church takes the credit to his church for the change of the Sabbath. Second, pressure is mounting for a reformed calendar.

It is true that the Vatican Council specified that its action was taken "providing this is agreeable to all others who are concerned with the problem, especially to other Christians." However, there is evidence that a movement is at work behind the scenes building opinion favoring a change of the calendar even if it should disrupt the cycle of the week. The fact is that it is not possible to have a perpetual calendar and at the same time maintain the weekly cycle.

Can we imagine the economic hardship on a wage earner who attempted to keep the creation Sabbath as it wandered through the week in a calendar with a blank day? It is not hard to visualize the confusion that would take place even in the ranks of Sabbath keepers should such a calendar be adopted. Perhaps this could be one of the means Satan will utilize to make his proud boast come true.

CONCLUSION

We have considered eleven prophecies. We have noted several ways in which these prophecies are being fulfilled. What more could a loving God do to warn His people of the approaching end?

The pioneers of this message preached with power the prophecies of the Word. They believed they would come to pass. If they could arise and see what we see, and hear what we hear, they would cry out in a mighty voice, "This is the hour of fulfilled prophecy! This is the time to lift up the voice as a trumpet, to sound the voice of the third angel, and to finish God's work!"

Earth's last hours are fast approaching. It is already late! What we do we must do quickly. Let us accept the wonderful provision God has made for personal cleansing from sin, and let us claim the power He has made available to witness for Him. The world needs to know these things. We are His heralds for announcing the last tremendous events that soon must come upon the world.